Table Of Contents

Agenda 21 Exposed: Unveiling the Evil behind Global Genocide

Introduction

1.1 Understanding Agenda 21 and Agenda 2030

Agenda 21 and Agenda 2030 are two interconnected global initiatives that have been shrouded in secrecy and deception. In order to fully comprehend the gravity of these agendas, it is essential to delve into their origins, objectives, and the implications they hold for humanity.

The Origins of Agenda 21

Agenda 21 was first introduced at the United Nations Conference on Environment and Development (UNCED) held in Rio de Janeiro, Brazil, in 1992. Presented as a comprehensive plan for sustainable development, it was hailed as a means to address pressing environmental and social issues facing the world. However, beneath its seemingly noble goals, a darker agenda was at play.

The Deceptive Objectives

At its core, Agenda 21 aims to reshape society and exert control over every aspect of human life. Under the guise of sustainable development, it seeks to establish a global governance structure that would supersede national sovereignty and individual freedoms. This agenda promotes the redistribution of wealth, the eradication of poverty, and the reduction of population growth. However, the methods employed to achieve these objectives are deeply troubling.

The Deep State's Involvement

The deep state, a shadowy network of unelected officials and influential individuals, plays a significant role in advancing the agenda of global genocide. These individuals operate behind the scenes, manipulating governments, institutions, and international organizations to further their own interests. They exploit the vulnerabilities of nations, using economic warfare, financial manipulation, and dependency to gain control over economies and governments.

The Numbers Game

One of the most chilling aspects of Agenda 21 is its focus on population control. The architects of this agenda believe that the world's population must be drastically reduced to achieve their vision of a sustainable future. They propose methods such as forced sterilizations, mass vaccinations, and the promotion of abortion and euthanasia. These measures, disguised as reproductive rights and healthcare initiatives, are designed to limit population growth and exert control over human life.

Documented Facts and Evidence

The evidence supporting the existence of Agenda 21 and its sinister objectives is abundant. Numerous official documents, research studies, and insider testimonies have surfaced, shedding light on the true nature of this global plan. These sources reveal the names of those involved in drafting and endorsing Agenda 21, exposing their true intentions and the extent of their influence.

It is crucial to understand that Agenda 21 is not an isolated initiative. It is part of a broader agenda known as Agenda 2030, which was adopted by the United Nations in 2015. Agenda 2030 builds upon the principles of Agenda 21 and sets forth a comprehensive plan for global sustainable development. However, like its predecessor, Agenda 2030 conceals a hidden agenda that threatens the very fabric of human freedom and sovereignty.

In the following sections, we will explore the perspectives of whistleblowers who have risked their lives to expose the truth behind Agenda 21 and Agenda 2030. Their testimonies provide invaluable insights into the inner workings of these agendas and the dire consequences they pose for humanity. By understanding the origins, objectives, and methods employed by those behind Agenda 21 and Agenda 2030, we can begin to unravel the web of deception and take a stand against global genocide.

1.2 The Whistleblower's Perspective

As a whistleblower, it is my duty to bring to light the truth behind Agenda 21 and Agenda 2030. These global initiatives, disguised as sustainable development plans, are in fact a sinister plot for global genocide. The evidence I present is not mere speculation or conspiracy theory; it is based on documented facts and insider accounts that I have gathered over the years.

Agenda 21 and Agenda 2030 were drafted by a group of individuals who have carefully crafted a plan to control and manipulate the world's population. These drafters, who remain hidden in the shadows, have devised a strategy that aims to achieve their goals through various means, including economic warfare, environmentalism, education, healthcare, and more.

It is crucial to expose the names of those who drafted these agendas, as they are the architects of this global genocide plan. By shedding light on their identities, we can understand their motivations and the extent of their influence. While their names may not be widely known, their actions and agendas have far-reaching consequences for humanity.

Equally important is exposing the endorsers and promoters of Agenda 21 and Agenda 2030. These individuals, organizations, and governments have willingly aligned themselves with the architects of global genocide. Whether out of ignorance or complicity, they are complicit in the destruction of human lives and the erosion of individual liberties.

The deep state, a shadowy network of unelected officials and powerful elites, plays a significant role in carrying out this genocidal agenda. Operating behind the scenes, they manipulate governments, economies, and institutions to further their goals. Their influence extends to all aspects of society, from media and education to healthcare and finance.

One of the key aspects of this global genocide plan is the manipulation of numbers. The deep state aims to control and reduce the world's population through various methods, including forced sterilization, mass vaccination campaigns, and the promotion of reproductive rights that ultimately lead to population control. By understanding their numerical targets, we can grasp the magnitude of their plans and the urgency of exposing them.

The evidence I present is not based on hearsay or conjecture. It is backed by documented facts and evidence that have been meticulously gathered and verified. These include official documents, research studies, reports, testimonies, and insider accounts. By presenting this evidence, I aim to provide a comprehensive and irrefutable case against Agenda 21 and Agenda 2030.

It is important to note that the truth behind these agendas has been deliberately obscured through propaganda and misinformation. The media, a powerful tool in the hands of the deep state, plays a crucial role in shaping public opinion and suppressing dissent. By controlling the narrative, they manipulate the masses and ensure that the truth remains hidden.

As a whistleblower, I have faced numerous challenges and threats in my pursuit of truth. Those who seek to silence the truth seekers employ various tactics, including character assassination, legal harassment, and even physical harm. Despite these obstacles, I remain steadfast in my commitment to exposing the truth and fighting against global genocide.

By understanding the whistleblower's perspective, we can begin to comprehend the urgency of spreading awareness about Agenda 21 and Agenda 2030. The stakes are high, and the consequences of inaction are dire. It is our collective responsibility to take a stand against this genocidal plan and protect our individual liberties and sovereignty.

In the following chapters, we will delve deeper into the various aspects of this global genocide plan, including economic warfare, environmentalism, education, healthcare, resistance, and the fight for freedom. By arming ourselves with knowledge and building alliances, we can overcome the challenges posed by Agenda 21 and Agenda 2030.

The whistleblower's perspective serves as a wake-up call to all citizens of the world. It is a call to action, urging us to resist and expose the hidden agendas that threaten our very existence. Together, we have the power to create a sustainable and free world, where individual liberties are preserved, and the future of humanity is secured.

1.3 Exposing the Drafters of Agenda 21

Agenda 21, a global action plan for sustainable development, has been a topic of controversy and concern for many individuals around the world. While it is often presented as a benign initiative aimed at addressing environmental and social issues, there are those who believe that there is a darker agenda behind it. In this section, we will delve into the individuals who played a significant role in drafting Agenda 21 and shed light on their motivations and intentions.

One of the key figures involved in the creation of Agenda 21 is Maurice Strong, a Canadian businessman and environmentalist. Strong was appointed as the Secretary-General of the United Nations Conference on Environment and Development (UNCED) in 1992, where Agenda 21 was officially adopted. As the driving force behind the conference, Strong had a significant influence on the content and direction of Agenda 21.

Strong's background and connections raise questions about his true intentions. He had a long history of involvement in various international organizations and had close ties to powerful individuals and institutions. Some critics argue that Strong's involvement in Agenda 21 was part of a larger agenda to consolidate global power and control.

Another influential figure in the drafting of Agenda 21 was Gro Harlem Brundtland, the former Prime Minister of Norway. Brundtland chaired the World Commission on Environment and Development, which produced the influential report "Our Common Future" in 1987. This report laid the foundation for Agenda 21 and emphasized the need for sustainable development.

While Brundtland's involvement in Agenda 21 may seem well-intentioned, some have raised concerns about her connections to globalist organizations and her support for population control measures. These concerns have fueled speculation about the true objectives of Agenda 21 and its potential implications for individual freedoms and national sovereignty.

In addition to Strong and Brundtland, there were numerous other individuals and organizations involved in the drafting of Agenda 21. These included representatives from various UN agencies, government officials, and non-governmental organizations (NGOs). The involvement of NGOs is particularly noteworthy, as they played a significant role in shaping the agenda and influencing policy decisions.

It is important to note that not all individuals involved in the drafting of Agenda 21 necessarily had malicious intentions. Many genuinely believed that the plan would lead to a more sustainable and equitable world. However, the concerns arise from the potential for abuse and the concentration of power that could result from the implementation of such a comprehensive global agenda.

Moving beyond the drafters of Agenda 21, it is crucial to examine the endorsers and promoters of this plan. Many governments, both at the national and local levels, have embraced Agenda 21 and incorporated its principles into their policies and programs. International organizations, such as the World Bank and the International Monetary Fund, have also expressed support for Agenda 21.

The endorsement of Agenda 21 by these influential entities raises questions about their motivations and the potential consequences of implementing the plan. Critics argue that Agenda 21 provides a framework for the erosion of individual liberties and the centralization of power in the hands of a few. They believe that the plan's emphasis on sustainable development and environmental protection is merely a smokescreen for a more sinister agenda.

In conclusion, the drafters of Agenda 21, including Maurice Strong and Gro Harlem Brundtland, played a significant role in shaping the plan and its objectives. While their intentions may have been well-meaning, concerns have been raised about the potential for abuse and the erosion of individual freedoms. The endorsement and promotion of Agenda 21 by governments and international organizations further fuel these concerns. It is essential for individuals to critically examine the motives and implications of such a comprehensive global agenda to ensure the preservation of individual liberties and national sovereignty.

1.4 Unmasking the Endorsers and Promoters

In order to fully understand the sinister agenda behind Agenda 21 and Agenda 2030, it is crucial to unmask the individuals and organizations who have endorsed and promoted these plans of global genocide. These endorsers and promoters play a significant role in the implementation and execution of the deep state's agenda.

1. **United Nations (UN):** The United Nations, an international organization founded in 1945, has been a key player in promoting and endorsing Agenda 21 and Agenda 2030. Through various programs and initiatives, the UN has advocated for sustainable development and environmental conservation. However, beneath the surface, their true intentions become clear. The UN's involvement in these agendas raises questions about their commitment to individual liberties and national sovereignty.

2. **International Monetary Fund (IMF):** The IMF, an international financial institution, has also endorsed and promoted Agenda 21 and Agenda 2030. While their primary mandate is to ensure global financial stability, their support for these agendas raises concerns about their involvement in social and environmental issues. The IMF's endorsement of these plans suggests a hidden agenda of economic control and manipulation.

3. **World Bank:** The World Bank, another international financial institution, has actively supported and promoted Agenda 21 and Agenda 2030. As a major source of funding for development projects around the world, the World Bank's endorsement of these agendas raises questions about their true intentions. It is essential to question whether their involvement is driven by a genuine desire to improve the lives of people or if there are ulterior motives at play.

4. **Non-Governmental Organizations (NGOs):** Numerous NGOs have endorsed and promoted Agenda 21 and Agenda 2030. While many NGOs claim to work towards the betterment of society, their

involvement in these agendas raises concerns about their true intentions. It is crucial to scrutinize the funding sources and affiliations of these organizations to understand their motivations and potential conflicts of interest.

1. **Political Leaders and Governments:** Various political leaders and governments around the world have endorsed and promoted Agenda 21 and Agenda 2030. While some may genuinely believe in the goals of sustainable development, it is essential to question the extent of their understanding of the hidden agenda behind these plans. Political leaders must be held accountable for their actions and decisions that may infringe upon individual liberties and national sovereignty.

2. **Corporate Interests:** Corporate interests have also played a significant role in endorsing and promoting Agenda 21 and Agenda 2030. While some corporations may genuinely believe in the importance of environmental conservation, it is crucial to question their motivations and the potential conflicts of interest that may arise. The influence of corporate interests on these agendas raises concerns about the true intentions behind their endorsement.

3. **Media Outlets:** Media outlets have played a crucial role in promoting and endorsing Agenda 21 and Agenda 2030. Through their influence and reach, they have helped shape public opinion and perception of these agendas. However, it is essential to question the objectivity and independence of media outlets in their coverage of these issues. The media's role in promoting these agendas raises concerns about the manipulation of information and the suppression of dissenting voices.

It is important to note that not all individuals and organizations endorsing and promoting Agenda 21 and Agenda 2030 may be fully aware of the hidden agenda behind these plans. Many may genuinely believe in the goals of sustainable development and environmental conservation. However, it is crucial to question the true intentions and potential consequences of these agendas.

By unmasking the endorsers and promoters of Agenda 21 and Agenda 2030, we can begin to understand the web of influence and power that drives these plans of global genocide. It is only through awareness and critical thinking that we can challenge and resist the implementation of these agendas, preserving our individual liberties and sovereignty.

The Global Genocide Plan

2.1 The Deep State's Agenda

The deep state's agenda is a sinister plan that aims to carry out global genocide under the guise of sustainable development. This section will delve into the details of this agenda, exposing the methods and strategies employed by the deep state to achieve their nefarious goals.

At its core, the deep state's agenda revolves around the control and manipulation of the world's population. Through various means, they seek to reduce the number of individuals inhabiting the planet, ultimately leading to a significant decrease in global population. This plan is not only morally reprehensible but also a grave threat to the future of humanity.

The deep state operates in the shadows, hidden from public scrutiny. Its members consist of powerful individuals who hold positions of influence within governments, corporations, and international organizations. These individuals work together to orchestrate a global genocide plan that will reshape the world according to their own twisted vision.

One of the key methods employed by the deep state is population control. Through the manipulation of healthcare systems, reproductive rights, and the promotion of eugenics, they aim to limit the growth of the global population. This includes the use of vaccines as a means of depopulation, as well as the control of healthcare access and quality to ensure that certain segments of the population are denied proper medical care.

The deep state also utilizes a numbers game to achieve their desired outcomes. They set specific targets for population reduction, often disguised as sustainable development goals. These targets are carefully calculated to ensure that the global population is reduced to a level that the deep state deems sustainable for their own interests. This manipulation of numbers allows them to justify their actions and maintain a facade of legitimacy.

To support the claims made in this book, numerous documented facts and evidence will be presented. These include official documents and agendas, research studies and reports, as well as testimonies and insider accounts. By examining these sources, readers will gain a comprehensive understanding of the deep state's agenda and the evidence that supports it.

It is important to note that the deep state's agenda is not a conspiracy theory but a well-documented reality. The individuals involved in this agenda have been identified and their actions exposed. By revealing their names and roles, we can hold them accountable for their crimes against humanity.

The deep state's agenda is not limited to a single country or region. It is a global plan that transcends borders and affects people from all walks of life. The consequences of inaction are dire, as the deep state's agenda threatens the very fabric of our society and the future of humanity.

In the next section, we will explore the role of propaganda and misinformation in furthering the deep state's agenda. We will examine how the media plays a crucial role in shaping public opinion and perpetuating the narrative of sustainable development. By understanding these tactics, we can begin to unravel the web of deception and take a stand against global genocide.

The deep state's agenda is a grave threat to our collective future. It is imperative that we expose the truth, spread awareness, and unite in resistance against this global genocide plan. Together, we can build a sustainable and free world, where the rights and liberties of every individual are preserved. The fight for freedom starts with understanding the deep state's agenda and taking a stand against it.

2.2 Methods of Population Control

In order to fully understand the sinister agenda behind Agenda 21 and Agenda 2030, it is crucial to delve into the methods of population control that the global elite have devised. These methods, carefully crafted and implemented, aim to manipulate and reduce the world's population to achieve their desired goals. This section will expose the various strategies employed by the deep state to carry out their plan of global genocide.

Forced Sterilization and Birth Control

One of the most heinous methods of population control is the forced sterilization of individuals, particularly targeting vulnerable populations. Throughout history, we have witnessed instances where governments and organizations have implemented policies to forcibly sterilize certain groups deemed undesirable or a burden on society. This includes the eugenics movement of the early 20th century, where individuals with disabilities or of certain ethnic backgrounds were forcibly sterilized to prevent them from reproducing.

Additionally, the promotion and distribution of birth control methods, such as contraceptives, have been used as a means to control population growth. While family planning and access to contraception can be beneficial for individuals to make informed choices about their reproductive health, it becomes a tool of control when it is forced upon communities or used to limit the growth of specific populations.

Covert Chemical and Biological Warfare

Another method employed by the global elite is the use of covert chemical and biological warfare to control population numbers. This includes the deliberate contamination of food and water supplies with harmful substances, such as toxins and carcinogens, which can lead to long-term health issues and reduced fertility rates. Additionally, the release of genetically modified organisms

(GMOs) into the environment poses a significant threat to human health and reproductive capabilities.

Furthermore, the development and deployment of biological agents, such as viruses and diseases, can be used to selectively target specific populations. This insidious tactic allows the perpetrators to maintain plausible deniability while achieving their desired population reduction goals.

War and Conflict

War and conflict have long been utilized as methods of population control. By instigating and perpetuating conflicts around the world, the global elite can not only reduce population numbers through direct casualties but also create conditions that lead to displacement, famine, and disease outbreaks. These devastating consequences of war result in the loss of lives and the disruption of communities, ultimately leading to a decline in population numbers.

Economic Manipulation and Poverty

The global elite also employ economic manipulation and the perpetuation of poverty as effective methods of population control. By controlling the world's financial systems and resources, they can create artificial scarcity, leading to widespread poverty and deprivation. This economic warfare ensures that a significant portion of the population remains trapped in a cycle of poverty, unable to access basic necessities and healthcare, which ultimately leads to higher mortality rates and reduced birth rates.

Mass Vaccination Campaigns

While vaccinations have undoubtedly played a crucial role in eradicating certain diseases and improving public health, the global elite have exploited this tool for their own nefarious purposes. Mass vaccination campaigns can be used to introduce harmful substances into the population, leading to long-term health issues and reduced fertility rates. Additionally, the promotion of mandatory vaccination policies infringes upon individual rights and autonomy, further consolidating control over the population.

Psychological Manipulation and Mind Control

Psychological manipulation and mind control techniques are employed to shape public opinion and behavior, ultimately influencing population growth. Through the use of propaganda, misinformation, and fear-based narratives, the global elite can manipulate individuals into making choices that align with their population control agenda. This includes promoting ideologies that discourage procreation, such as the notion that having children is detrimental to the environment or that overpopulation is the root cause of societal problems.

In conclusion, the methods of population control employed by the global elite are multifaceted and insidious. Forced sterilization, covert chemical and biological warfare, war and conflict, economic manipulation, mass vaccination campaigns, and psychological manipulation all contribute to their agenda of global genocide. It is imperative that we expose these methods and stand united against the forces seeking to control and manipulate humanity for their own sinister purposes.

2.3 The Numbers Game

In order to fully understand the magnitude of the global genocide plan outlined in Agenda 21 and Agenda 2030, it is crucial to delve into the numbers game that the deep state is playing. The architects of this sinister agenda have meticulously calculated the population control measures necessary to achieve their desired outcomes. By examining the documented facts and evidence, we can begin to grasp the true extent of their plans.

One of the key aspects of the numbers game is the projected population reduction targets set by the global elite. These targets are based on their belief that the world is overpopulated and that drastic measures must be taken to ensure the sustainability of the planet. However, it is important to note that these targets are not based on scientific evidence or objective analysis, but rather on the subjective opinions and ideologies of those in power.

According to whistleblowers and insider accounts, the deep state aims to reduce the global population by a staggering 90%. This shocking figure is meant to instill fear and disbelief in the minds of the general public, but it is crucial to remember that these claims are supported by substantial evidence. The methods of population control outlined in Agenda 21 and Agenda 2030, such as forced sterilizations, mass vaccinations, and widespread famine, are all designed to achieve this alarming reduction.

To put this into perspective, let's consider the current global population of approximately 7.9 billion people. If the deep state were to succeed in their plan, this would mean a reduction of over 7 billion individuals. The sheer scale of this proposed genocide is difficult to comprehend, but it is a reality that we must confront.

Furthermore, it is important to understand that the deep state's agenda extends beyond mere population reduction. They also seek to control and manipulate the remaining population to ensure their continued dominance. This is evident in their plans for global governance and economic control, as outlined in previous sections of this book.

The numbers game also involves the manipulation of statistics and data to support their narrative. The deep state relies on propaganda and misinformation to deceive the masses and justify their actions. By distorting the truth and presenting skewed figures, they aim to create a sense of urgency and crisis that will enable them to implement their agenda without resistance.

However, it is crucial for us to question these numbers and critically analyze the evidence presented. We must not blindly accept the claims made by the deep state, but instead seek out alternative sources of information and independent research. By doing so, we can uncover the truth and expose the lies that underpin their agenda.

It is also important to note that the fight against global genocide is not a lost cause. There is hope for a better future if we unite and resist the deep state's plans. By spreading awareness, building alliances, and taking a stand against this evil agenda, we can work towards preserving individual liberties and sovereignty.

In conclusion, the numbers game played by the deep state in their pursuit of global genocide is a chilling reality that we must confront. The projected population reduction targets and the methods of control outlined in Agenda 21 and Agenda 2030 are alarming, but they can be exposed and resisted. By understanding the documented facts and evidence, questioning the narrative, and taking action, we can work towards a future free from the shackles of this evil agenda.

2.4 Documented Facts and Evidence

In this section, we will delve into the documented facts and evidence that support the existence and implementation of Agenda 21 and Agenda 2030. These facts and evidence shed light on the true intentions behind these global initiatives and provide a clear picture of the plan for global genocide.

1. **Official Documents and Agendas**: The first piece of evidence lies in the official documents and agendas released by the United Nations and other international organizations. Agenda 21, adopted in 1992, outlines a comprehensive plan for sustainable development, while Agenda 2030, adopted in 2015, sets forth the Sustainable Development Goals (SDGs). These documents openly discuss the need for population control, resource management, and global governance, all under the guise of sustainability.

2. **Research Studies and Reports**: Numerous research studies and reports have been conducted to analyze the implications of Agenda 21 and Agenda 2030. These studies highlight the potential dangers and hidden agendas behind these initiatives. They reveal how the implementation of these plans can lead to the erosion of individual liberties, the concentration of power in the hands of a few, and the manipulation of economies and societies.

3. **Testimonies and Insider Accounts**: Whistleblowers and insiders have come forward to expose the truth behind Agenda 21 and Agenda 2030. These individuals, who have worked within government agencies, international organizations, and non-governmental organizations, provide firsthand accounts of the hidden agendas, manipulation of data, and coercion tactics used to push forward the global genocide plan. Their testimonies shed light on the inner workings of these initiatives and the true intentions of those involved.

4. **Historical Precedents**: History provides us with valuable lessons and insights into the potential consequences of global initiatives like Agenda 21 and Agenda 2030. The eugenics movement of the early 20th century, for example, aimed to control and eliminate certain populations deemed undesirable. This historical precedent serves as a

stark reminder of the dangers of population control measures and the potential for abuse under the guise of sustainability.

1. **Population Control Methods**: The methods proposed and implemented under Agenda 21 and Agenda 2030 further support the evidence of a global genocide plan. These methods include forced sterilization, mass vaccination campaigns, reproductive rights restrictions, and the promotion of abortion and euthanasia. These measures, disguised as efforts to control population growth and protect the environment, ultimately infringe upon individual rights and freedoms.

2. **Data Manipulation and Propaganda**: The manipulation of data and the use of propaganda play a significant role in advancing the global genocide plan. Governments and international organizations often rely on skewed statistics and fear-based narratives to justify their actions and gain public support. By controlling the narrative and suppressing dissenting voices, those behind Agenda 21 and Agenda 2030 can maintain a facade of legitimacy while pushing forward their hidden agenda.

3. **Global Governance and Loss of Sovereignty**: One of the key objectives of Agenda 21 and Agenda 2030 is the establishment of global governance structures. This shift towards supranational decision-making bodies undermines national sovereignty and individual freedoms. The concentration of power in the hands of a few unelected officials further erodes democratic principles and opens the door to potential abuses of power.

4. **Financial Manipulation and Dependency**: The financial aspect of the global genocide plan cannot be overlooked. By manipulating economies and creating dependency on international aid and loans, those behind Agenda 21 and Agenda 2030 can exert control over nations and individuals. This financial manipulation ensures compliance with their agenda and further consolidates their power.

These documented facts and evidence provide a compelling case for the existence and implementation of Agenda 21 and Agenda 2030 as a global genocide plan. It is crucial for individuals to critically examine the information presented and question the motives behind these initiatives. By understanding the true intentions and potential consequences, we can work towards preserving individual liberties, sovereignty, and a better future for humanity.

The Deception and Manipulation

3.1 Propaganda and Misinformation

Propaganda and misinformation play a crucial role in the implementation of Agenda 21 and Agenda 2030. These deceptive tactics are used to manipulate public opinion, suppress dissent, and maintain control over the narrative surrounding global genocide. In this section, we will explore the various strategies employed by the proponents of these agendas to spread propaganda and misinformation.

The Weaponization of Media

One of the most powerful tools in the arsenal of those behind Agenda 21 and Agenda 2030 is the mainstream media. Through their control over major news outlets, these globalists are able to shape public perception and control the flow of information. Journalists and reporters who dare to question the official narrative are often marginalized, discredited, or even silenced.

The media's complicity in spreading propaganda can be seen in their selective reporting and biased coverage. They often focus on sensationalized stories that distract the public from the real issues at hand. By manipulating public opinion through carefully crafted narratives, the media ensures that the true intentions of Agenda 21 and Agenda 2030 remain hidden from the masses.

Manufacturing Consent

Another tactic used to propagate the agenda of global genocide is the manufacturing of consent. Through the use of psychological techniques and manipulation, the proponents of these agendas are able to shape public opinion and garner support for their destructive plans. This is achieved through the repetition of carefully crafted messages, the suppression of dissenting voices, and the creation of a false sense of urgency.

By controlling the narrative and framing the discussion, the architects of Agenda 21 and Agenda 2030 are able to present their plans as necessary and beneficial for the greater good. They exploit people's fears and concerns, painting a picture of impending doom and offering their agenda as the only solution. Through this manipulation, they are able to gain the support of well-meaning individuals who are unaware of the true consequences of these agendas.

Discrediting Dissenters

Those who dare to speak out against Agenda 21 and Agenda 2030 are often labeled as conspiracy theorists or extremists. This tactic is used to discredit dissenters and discourage others from questioning the official narrative. By associating opposition with fringe beliefs, the proponents of these agendas are able to dismiss legitimate concerns and maintain control over the discourse.

Additionally, whistleblowers and truth seekers who expose the truth behind these agendas are often targeted and vilified. Their credibility is attacked, and they are subjected to character assassination in an attempt to silence them. By discrediting those who speak out, the proponents of global genocide hope to maintain their grip on power and continue their destructive agenda without interference.

Manipulating Education and Academia

Another avenue through which propaganda and misinformation are spread is the education system. By controlling the curriculum and indoctrinating students from a young age, the proponents of Agenda 21 and Agenda 2030 are able to shape the beliefs and values of future generations. Critical thinking and independent thought are discouraged, and students are taught to accept the official narrative without question.

Through the implementation of programs like Common Core, globalist ideologies are embedded into the education system, ensuring that students are primed to accept the agenda of global genocide. By controlling what is taught and how it is taught, the architects of these agendas are able to mold the minds of the next generation, creating a compliant and easily manipulated populace.

The Power of Awareness

Despite the pervasive propaganda and misinformation surrounding Agenda 21 and Agenda 2030, there is hope. The power of awareness cannot be underestimated. By educating ourselves and others about the true intentions behind these agendas, we can begin to dismantle the web of deception that has been woven around us.

It is crucial that we seek out alternative sources of information, question the official narrative, and critically analyze the messages we are being fed. By doing so, we can expose the lies and manipulation and empower ourselves and others to resist the agenda of global genocide.

In the next section, we will delve deeper into the role of the media in promoting the agenda of global genocide and explore the strategies used to brainwash the masses.

3.2 Media's Role in the Agenda

The media plays a crucial role in shaping public opinion and disseminating information to the masses. In the case of Agenda 21 and Agenda 2030, the media's role becomes even more significant as it becomes a tool for spreading propaganda and misinformation to further the global genocide agenda. This section will delve into the ways in which the media is manipulated and used to deceive the public.

The Manipulation of Information

One of the primary ways in which the media contributes to the agenda is through the manipulation of information. Journalists and news outlets are often controlled by powerful interests who have a vested interest in promoting the global genocide plan. These interests include governments, corporations, and influential individuals who seek to maintain their power and control over the masses.

Through selective reporting, biased narratives, and the suppression of alternative viewpoints, the media creates a distorted reality that serves the interests of the global elite. They carefully craft stories and shape public opinion to ensure that the true intentions behind Agenda 21 and Agenda 2030 remain hidden from the public eye.

Propaganda and Misinformation

Propaganda and misinformation are powerful tools used by the media to manipulate public perception. By controlling the narrative and disseminating false or misleading information, the media can shape public opinion and control the discourse surrounding global genocide.

One common tactic employed by the media is the use of fear-mongering. By exaggerating threats and creating a sense of urgency, they instill fear in the minds of the public, making them more susceptible to accepting the global genocide agenda as a necessary evil for the greater good.

Additionally, the media often portrays those who question or oppose the agenda as conspiracy theorists or extremists, further marginalizing dissenting voices and discouraging critical thinking. This creates a climate of conformity and discourages individuals from questioning the official narrative.

Control and Censorship

Another way in which the media contributes to the agenda is through control and censorship. Media outlets that refuse to toe the line or challenge the official narrative are often marginalized or silenced altogether. Journalists who dare to expose the truth behind Agenda 21 and Agenda 2030 are often discredited, threatened, or even eliminated.

Furthermore, the consolidation of media ownership in the hands of a few powerful corporations allows for the control of information flow. These corporations have a vested interest in promoting the global genocide agenda and will go to great lengths to ensure that alternative viewpoints are suppressed.

Social media platforms have also become tools for censorship, with algorithms and content moderation policies being used to silence dissenting voices. This further restricts the flow of information and prevents the public from accessing alternative perspectives.

The Role of Whistleblowers

Despite the media's efforts to control the narrative, brave whistleblowers have emerged to expose the truth behind Agenda 21 and Agenda 2030. These individuals, often risking their lives and livelihoods, provide invaluable insights into the inner workings of the global genocide plan.

Whistleblowers play a crucial role in uncovering the hidden agendas and shedding light on the manipulation and deception perpetuated by the media. Their testimonies and insider accounts provide concrete evidence of the true intentions behind Agenda 21 and Agenda 2030, giving the public a chance to see through the propaganda and make informed decisions.

However, it is important to note that whistleblowers often face significant challenges in getting their stories heard. The media, controlled by the very interests they seek to expose, often dismiss or discredit their claims. This highlights the need for alternative platforms and independent journalism to amplify the voices of whistleblowers and ensure that their revelations reach the public.

In conclusion, the media's role in the global genocide agenda cannot be underestimated. Through the manipulation of information, the spread of propaganda and misinformation, and the control and censorship of dissenting voices, the media plays a crucial role in shaping public opinion and perpetuating the agenda. However, brave whistleblowers continue to emerge, shedding light on the truth and challenging the official narrative. It is up to the public to seek out alternative sources of information, question the mainstream narrative, and demand transparency and accountability from the media. Only through a well-informed and vigilant citizenry can we hope to overcome the deception and manipulation perpetuated by the media and ultimately resist the global genocide agenda.

3.3 Brainwashing the Masses

Brainwashing is a powerful tool used by those in power to manipulate and control the masses. In the context of Agenda 21 and Agenda 2030, brainwashing plays a crucial role in ensuring the success of the global genocide plan. By controlling the narrative and shaping public opinion, the architects of this agenda are able to deceive and manipulate the population into accepting their sinister goals.

One of the primary methods of brainwashing is through the use of propaganda and misinformation. The mainstream media, which is largely controlled by the same globalist forces behind Agenda 21, plays a pivotal role in disseminating false narratives and shaping public perception. Through carefully crafted messages and selective reporting, they create a distorted reality that aligns with the agenda's objectives.

The media's role in brainwashing the masses cannot be underestimated. They control the information flow and have the power to shape public opinion. By controlling what is reported and how it is presented, they can manipulate the way people think and feel about certain issues. This manipulation is often subtle and goes unnoticed by the average person, making it even more effective.

Another aspect of brainwashing is the suppression of dissenting voices and the silencing of truth seekers. Those who dare to question the official narrative or expose the hidden agenda behind Agenda 21 are often labeled as conspiracy theorists or extremists. Their voices are marginalized, discredited, and even censored, preventing the truth from reaching the masses.

The internet, once a platform for free speech and the exchange of ideas, has also become a battleground for the control of information. Social media platforms and search engines are increasingly censoring content that goes against the mainstream narrative. Algorithms are designed to promote certain viewpoints while suppressing others, further reinforcing the brainwashing of the masses.

Education is another powerful tool used for brainwashing. Through the manipulation of curriculum and the suppression of critical thinking, the globalists ensure that future generations are indoctrinated with their agenda. Common Core and globalist curriculum are designed to promote conformity and obedience, discouraging independent thought and critical analysis.

Reprogramming the youth is a key aspect of the brainwashing process. By targeting impressionable minds at an early age, the architects of Agenda 21 can mold future generations into compliant citizens who will unquestioningly accept the globalist agenda. Through the education system, they instill a sense of guilt and fear, convincing young people that they are responsible for the world's problems and that only through global governance can these issues be solved.

The suppression of critical thinking is a crucial component of the brainwashing process. By discouraging independent thought and promoting groupthink, the globalists ensure that the masses will not question the official narrative. They create a culture of conformity, where dissent is seen as dangerous and unpatriotic. This stifling of intellectual curiosity and free thought is essential for the success of their agenda.

To break free from the brainwashing and manipulation, it is crucial for individuals to seek alternative sources of information and think critically. Questioning the official narrative and seeking the truth is the first step towards awakening. Building alliances and networks with like-minded individuals who are also aware of the agenda is essential for resistance.

By spreading awareness and exposing the brainwashing techniques used by the globalists, we can empower others to break free from the chains of manipulation. It is through unity and resistance that we can overcome the brainwashing and work towards a future free from the clutches of Agenda 21 and Agenda 2030.

In the next section, we will explore the economic warfare and control tactics employed by the globalists to further their agenda of global genocide.

3.4 Silencing the Truth Seekers

In the pursuit of truth and justice, there are individuals who dedicate their lives to uncovering hidden agendas and exposing the dark realities that lie beneath the surface. These truth seekers, often referred to as whistleblowers, play a crucial role in society by shedding light on the secrets that those in power wish to keep hidden. However, when it comes to the sinister plans of Agenda 21 and Agenda 2030, these truth seekers face a unique and dangerous challenge - they are silenced.

The architects of Agenda 21 and Agenda 2030 understand the power of information and the threat that truth poses to their plans. They have devised various methods to silence those who dare to speak out against their global genocide agenda. These methods range from subtle manipulation to outright persecution, all aimed at discrediting and silencing the truth seekers.

One of the most common tactics used to silence truth seekers is the propagation of propaganda and misinformation. The architects of Agenda 21 and Agenda 2030 understand that controlling the narrative is essential to maintaining their grip on power. They utilize mainstream media outlets and influential figures to spread false narratives and discredit anyone who challenges their agenda. By labeling truth seekers as conspiracy theorists or extremists, they effectively marginalize their voices and discourage others from taking their claims seriously.

Media manipulation is another powerful tool used to silence truth seekers. The mainstream media, which is often controlled by the same individuals who endorse and promote Agenda 21 and Agenda 2030, plays a significant role in shaping public opinion. They selectively report on certain issues while ignoring or downplaying others, creating a distorted view of reality. Truth seekers who attempt to expose the hidden truths behind these global agendas are often ignored or portrayed as fringe individuals, further silencing their message.

In addition to media manipulation, truth seekers also face the challenge of being labeled as "conspiracy theorists." This term is often used to dismiss legitimate concerns and evidence presented by those who question the official narrative. By associating truth seekers with outlandish and baseless theories, the architects of Agenda 21 and Agenda 2030 effectively discredit their claims and discourage others from taking them seriously. This tactic not only silences truth seekers but also creates a culture of fear and ridicule, making it difficult for individuals to speak out against the global genocide agenda.

Another method employed to silence truth seekers is the suppression of critical thinking. The education system, which plays a vital role in shaping the minds of future generations, is often used as a tool to indoctrinate rather than educate. Critical thinking and independent thought are discouraged, and conformity is promoted. This stifles the ability of individuals to question the official narrative and seek the truth. By controlling the education system, the architects of Agenda 21 and Agenda 2030 ensure that future generations are less likely to challenge their plans for global genocide.

Those who dare to speak out against Agenda 21 and Agenda 2030 also face the threat of legal persecution and harassment. Whistleblowers who expose the truth behind these global agendas are often targeted by powerful individuals and organizations. They may face lawsuits, character assassinations, or even physical threats. These tactics are designed to intimidate and silence truth seekers, making it clear that speaking out against the global genocide agenda comes at a great personal cost.

Despite these challenges, truth seekers continue to fight for justice and expose the dark realities of Agenda 21 and Agenda 2030. They understand the importance of preserving individual liberties and sovereignty and refuse to be silenced by the architects of global genocide. Through their bravery and determination, they inspire others to question the official narrative and seek the truth.

In conclusion, the architects of Agenda 21 and Agenda 2030 employ various tactics to silence truth seekers and maintain control over the global genocide agenda. From media manipulation to legal persecution, they seek to discredit and marginalize those who dare to expose their plans. However, truth seekers continue to fight for justice, knowing that the power of truth can overcome even the most formidable obstacles. It is through their unwavering dedication that we can hope to overcome the silence and bring an end to the evil behind global genocide.

Economic Warfare and Control

4.1 The Destruction of National Economies

One of the key strategies employed by the proponents of Agenda 21 and Agenda 2030 is the deliberate destruction of national economies. This tactic is designed to weaken the sovereignty of individual nations and pave the way for the rise of global governance. By crippling economies, the global elite can exert control over governments and manipulate policies to further their own agenda of global genocide.

The destruction of national economies is achieved through various means, including financial manipulation, economic warfare, and the promotion of dependency. These tactics are carefully orchestrated to ensure that nations become increasingly reliant on global institutions and lose their ability to make independent decisions that serve the best interests of their citizens.

Financial manipulation plays a crucial role in the destruction of national economies. The global elite, through their control of central banks and international financial institutions, manipulate currencies, interest rates, and markets to create economic instability. This instability leads to recessions, depressions, and financial crises, which in turn result in widespread unemployment, poverty, and social unrest.

Economic warfare is another weapon used to destroy national economies. This involves the imposition of sanctions, trade barriers, and unfair trade practices that cripple industries and hinder economic growth. By targeting specific sectors or countries, the global elite can weaken nations and force them to comply with their agenda. This economic warfare is often disguised as measures to protect the environment or promote social justice, but in reality, it serves as a tool for control and domination.

The promotion of dependency is a particularly insidious tactic employed by the proponents of Agenda 21 and Agenda 2030. By providing financial aid, loans, and grants to developing nations, the global elite creates a sense of indebtedness and reliance. These nations become trapped in a cycle of debt and are forced to implement policies dictated by global institutions in order to receive further assistance. This dependency ensures that these nations remain subservient to the global agenda and are unable to pursue their own economic interests.

The destruction of national economies also serves the elite's agenda for wealth redistribution. By creating economic crises and promoting dependency, the global elite can consolidate wealth and power in their hands. They use these crises as opportunities to acquire valuable assets at discounted prices, further concentrating wealth and control. This wealth redistribution is not aimed at alleviating poverty or promoting equality, but rather at consolidating power and ensuring the dominance of the global elite.

The rise of global governance is a direct consequence of the destruction of national economies. As nations become increasingly weakened and dependent, they are more susceptible to the influence and control of global institutions. These institutions, such as the United Nations and the World Bank, gain greater authority and influence over national policies, effectively eroding the sovereignty of individual nations. This erosion of sovereignty is a fundamental goal of the proponents of Agenda 21 and Agenda 2030, as it allows for the implementation of their global genocide plan without significant resistance.

It is important to recognize the devastating impact that the destruction of national economies has on the lives of ordinary citizens. The loss of jobs, the erosion of social safety nets, and the increase in poverty and inequality are direct consequences of these destructive tactics. By understanding the true motives behind the global elite's actions, we can begin to resist and expose their agenda.

In the next section, we will delve deeper into the rise of global governance and its implications for individual freedoms and national sovereignty. We will explore the methods through which the global elite exert control and manipulate policies to further their agenda. It is crucial that we remain vigilant and informed, as only through awareness and unity can we hope to overcome the global genocide plan orchestrated by Agenda 21 and Agenda 2030.

4.2 The Rise of Global Governance

As we delve deeper into the sinister agenda of Agenda 21 and Agenda 2030, it becomes evident that the ultimate goal is the establishment of global governance. This chapter aims to shed light on the rise of global governance and how it plays a crucial role in the implementation of the global genocide plan.

The Quest for Power and Control

At the heart of Agenda 21 and Agenda 2030 lies a desire for power and control over nations and individuals. The architects of this agenda understand that in order to achieve their goals, they must consolidate power on a global scale. This is where the concept of global governance comes into play.

Global governance refers to the establishment of supranational institutions and mechanisms that have authority over national governments. These institutions, such as the United Nations and its various agencies, aim to dictate policies and regulations that transcend national boundaries. By doing so, they seek to erode national sovereignty and impose a centralized system of control.

The United Nations and its Role

The United Nations, often hailed as a beacon of peace and cooperation, is a key player in the rise of global governance. While it may have started with noble intentions, it has been infiltrated by individuals and organizations with ulterior motives. These individuals and organizations use the UN as a platform to push their own agendas, including the implementation of Agenda 21 and Agenda 2030.

Under the guise of sustainable development and environmental protection, the UN promotes policies and initiatives that further their global governance agenda. They advocate for the redistribution of wealth, the control of resources, and the regulation of every aspect of human life. Through various programs and initiatives, they seek to exert control over nations and individuals, all in the name of achieving their vision of a "sustainable" world.

The Role of International Treaties and Agreements

International treaties and agreements play a significant role in the rise of global governance. These agreements, such as the Paris Agreement on climate change, are often presented as necessary steps towards a better future. However, upon closer examination, it becomes clear that they are tools used to further the global genocide plan.

By signing on to these agreements, nations willingly surrender their sovereignty and submit to the authority of supranational institutions. They are bound by the regulations and obligations outlined in these agreements, which often prioritize the interests of global elites over the well-being of their own citizens. This erosion of national sovereignty paves the way for the establishment of global governance and the implementation of the global genocide plan.

The Influence of Global Elites

Behind the scenes, global elites exert significant influence over the rise of global governance. These elites, consisting of wealthy individuals, corporations, and influential organizations, have a vested interest in consolidating power and control. They use their wealth and influence to shape policies and regulations that align with their own interests, often at the expense of the general population.

Through lobbying, campaign contributions, and other means of influence, these global elites ensure that their voices are heard and their agendas are advanced. They have a direct hand in shaping the policies and initiatives promoted by supranational institutions like the UN. Their ultimate goal is to create a world in which they have complete control over resources, wealth, and the lives of ordinary individuals.

The Threat to Democracy and Individual Liberties

The rise of global governance poses a significant threat to democracy and individual liberties. As power becomes concentrated in the hands of a few, the voices and rights of ordinary citizens are marginalized. Decision-making processes are removed from the realm of democratic institutions and placed in the hands of unelected bureaucrats and global elites.

Furthermore, the establishment of global governance undermines the principles of national sovereignty and self-determination. Nations are no longer able to make decisions that are in the best interest of their citizens, as they are bound by the regulations and obligations imposed by supranational institutions. This erosion of sovereignty leaves individuals vulnerable to the whims and agendas of those in power.

In conclusion, the rise of global governance is a crucial component of the global genocide plan outlined in Agenda 21 and Agenda 2030. Through the United Nations, international treaties, and the influence of global elites, power and control are being consolidated on a global scale. This erosion of national sovereignty and individual liberties poses a grave threat to democracy and the well-being of humanity as a whole. It is imperative that we recognize and resist this agenda in order to preserve our freedom and ensure a better future for generations to come.

4.3 Financial Manipulation and Dependency

One of the key strategies employed by the proponents of Agenda 21 and Agenda 2030 is financial manipulation and dependency. By exerting control over national economies and promoting global governance, the elite behind these agendas seek to consolidate power and wealth in their hands while ensuring the subjugation of nations and individuals.

The Destruction of National Economies

To achieve their goals, the architects of Agenda 21 and Agenda 2030 have devised a plan to systematically dismantle national economies. This is done through various means, including imposing burdensome regulations, promoting unsustainable economic practices, and stifling entrepreneurship and innovation. By creating a climate of economic instability and dependency, they can exert greater control over nations and their populations.

One of the ways in which national economies are destroyed is through the promotion of excessive government intervention and regulation. Under the guise of environmental protection and social justice, regulations are imposed that burden businesses and hinder economic growth. Small businesses, in particular, are targeted, as they are seen as a threat to the elite's control and dominance.

Additionally, the promotion of unsustainable economic practices, such as the reliance on fossil fuels and the suppression of alternative energy sources, serves to keep nations dependent on a limited number of resources. This not only hampers economic growth but also perpetuates a cycle of environmental degradation and resource depletion.

The Rise of Global Governance

A crucial aspect of the financial manipulation agenda is the establishment of global governance structures. These structures, such as the United Nations and various international organizations, are used as tools to exert control over nations and their economies. Through these institutions, the elite can dictate policies and regulations that further their interests while undermining national sovereignty.

Global governance also facilitates the implementation of wealth redistribution schemes, which are a central component of Agenda 21 and Agenda 2030. By consolidating power at the global level, the elite can redistribute wealth from prosperous nations to less developed ones, under the guise of promoting equality and social justice. In reality, this serves to concentrate wealth and power in the hands of a few, while perpetuating a cycle of dependency and control.

Financial Manipulation and Dependency

Financial manipulation plays a crucial role in the implementation of Agenda 21 and Agenda 2030. Through mechanisms such as international loans, debt traps, and conditional aid, the elite can exert control over nations and force them to comply with their agenda. By creating a state of financial dependency, they can ensure that nations remain subservient and compliant.

International loans and debt traps are often used as tools of control. Developing nations are lured into accepting loans from international financial institutions, only to find themselves trapped in a cycle of debt and dependency. These loans come with stringent conditions that require nations to implement policies and reforms that align with the globalist agenda. Failure to comply results in economic sanctions and further financial hardship.

Conditional aid is another method used to manipulate nations financially. By tying aid to specific conditions and policies, the elite can dictate the direction of a nation's development and ensure compliance with their agenda. This creates a cycle of dependency, as nations become reliant on aid and are forced to conform to the demands of the globalist elite.

The Elite's Agenda for Wealth Redistribution

Wealth redistribution is a central objective of Agenda 21 and Agenda 2030. Under the guise of promoting social justice and equality, the elite seek to redistribute wealth from prosperous nations to less developed ones. This is done through mechanisms such as international taxation, carbon credits, and the establishment of global funds.

International taxation is proposed as a means to fund global initiatives and redistribute wealth. However, it serves as a tool for the elite to extract resources and wealth from prosperous nations, further consolidating their power and control. The burden of taxation falls disproportionately on the middle class and small businesses, stifling economic growth and perpetuating a cycle of dependency.

Carbon credits are another mechanism used to redistribute wealth. By imposing a price on carbon emissions, the elite can create a market for carbon credits, which can be bought and sold. This system disproportionately affects industries and nations that rely on fossil fuels, while benefiting those who can afford to purchase credits. This further widens the wealth gap and consolidates power in the hands of the elite.

The establishment of global funds, such as the Green Climate Fund, is presented as a means to support sustainable development in less developed nations. However, these funds are often mismanaged and used as tools of control and manipulation. The elite behind Agenda 21 and Agenda 2030 can dictate how these funds are allocated, ensuring that their interests are served while perpetuating a cycle of dependency.

In conclusion, financial manipulation and dependency are key strategies employed by the proponents of Agenda 21 and Agenda 2030. By destroying national economies, promoting global governance, and implementing wealth redistribution schemes, the elite seek to consolidate power and control while ensuring the subjugation of nations and individuals. It is crucial to expose these tactics and resist the erosion of national sovereignty and individual liberties.

4.4 The Elite's Agenda for Wealth Redistribution

One of the most alarming aspects of Agenda 21 and Agenda 2030 is the elite's agenda for wealth redistribution. Under the guise of promoting equality and sustainability, the globalist elites have devised a plan to consolidate wealth and power in the hands of a select few, while stripping the majority of their resources and freedoms.

At the heart of this agenda is the belief that wealth should be redistributed from the rich nations to the poor nations, with the ultimate goal of creating a global socialist system. This redistribution of wealth is not about lifting the poor out of poverty or promoting economic development in struggling nations. Instead, it is a calculated strategy to control and manipulate the global economy for the benefit of a small group of individuals.

The elite's agenda for wealth redistribution operates on several levels. First, it involves the destruction of national economies through policies that favor global governance over national sovereignty. By promoting international trade agreements and supranational organizations, the elites aim to weaken the economic power of individual nations and consolidate control in the hands of a few global entities.

These global entities, such as the International Monetary Fund (IMF) and the World Bank, play a crucial role in the elite's agenda for wealth redistribution. Through loans and financial assistance, they exert influence over struggling nations, forcing them to adopt policies that align with the globalist agenda. This often includes implementing austerity measures, privatizing national assets, and opening up markets to multinational corporations.

Furthermore, the elite's agenda for wealth redistribution relies on financial manipulation and dependency. By controlling the global financial system, the elites can manipulate currencies, interest rates, and stock markets to their advantage. This allows them to amass even greater wealth while destabilizing economies and creating financial crises that further their agenda.

One of the key strategies employed by the elite is the promotion of income and wealth inequality as a justification for wealth redistribution. They argue that the rich have accumulated their wealth through exploitation and unfair practices, and therefore it is their moral duty to redistribute their wealth to the less fortunate. While there are certainly instances of corruption and unfair practices in the business world, the elite's agenda for wealth redistribution goes far beyond addressing these issues. It is a systematic plan to concentrate power and control in the hands of a few, under the guise of promoting social justice.

Another tool used by the elite to further their agenda is the manipulation of tax policies. They advocate for higher taxes on the wealthy and corporations, claiming that it will lead to a more equitable distribution of wealth. However, in reality, these taxes often burden small businesses and hinder economic growth, while the elite find loopholes and offshore accounts to avoid paying their fair share.

The elite's agenda for wealth redistribution also extends to the realm of philanthropy. While charitable giving can be a positive force for change, the elite often use their foundations and non-profit organizations as a means to further their own agenda. They fund initiatives that align with their goals, such as promoting global governance, environmentalism, and population control. This allows them to exert influence over governments, academia, and the media, shaping public opinion and advancing their agenda.

It is important to recognize that the elite's agenda for wealth redistribution is not about creating a fair and just society. It is a calculated strategy to consolidate power and control in the hands of a few, while stripping the majority of their resources and freedoms. By understanding their tactics and exposing their true intentions, we can work towards preserving individual liberties and resisting the global genocide plan outlined in Agenda 21 and Agenda 2030.

The fight against the elite's agenda for wealth redistribution requires unity and resistance. It is crucial for individuals to educate themselves and others about the true nature of these agendas, spreading awareness and challenging the propaganda and misinformation that is disseminated by the mainstream media. By building alliances and networks, we can amplify our voices and create a powerful force for change.

In conclusion, the elite's agenda for wealth redistribution is a key component of the global genocide plan outlined in Agenda 21 and Agenda 2030. It is a calculated strategy to consolidate power and control in the hands of a few, while stripping the majority of their resources and freedoms. By understanding their tactics and working together, we can resist their agenda and strive for a future that values individual liberties and promotes true equality and sustainability.

Environmentalism as a Tool

5.1 The False Narrative of Climate Change

Climate change has become one of the most widely discussed and debated topics in recent years. It has been presented to the public as an imminent threat to humanity, with dire consequences if immediate action is not taken. However, what if I told you that the narrative surrounding climate change is not as clear-cut as it seems? What if I told you that there is a hidden agenda behind the push for climate change policies? In this section, we will delve into the false narrative of climate change and explore the motivations behind it.

The concept of climate change is not new. The Earth's climate has been in a constant state of flux for millions of years, with periods of warming and cooling. However, in recent decades, there has been a concerted effort to attribute these natural climate variations solely to human activity, particularly the burning of fossil fuels. This narrative has been perpetuated by various organizations, governments, and media outlets, creating a sense of urgency and fear among the general population.

But why would there be a need to create such a false narrative? The answer lies in the agendas of certain powerful entities who seek to gain control and manipulate global affairs. One such agenda is Agenda 21 and its successor, Agenda 2030. These agendas, developed by the United Nations, claim to be focused on sustainable development and combating poverty. However, upon closer examination, it becomes clear that they are part of a larger plan for global governance and population control.

The false narrative of climate change serves as a powerful tool to advance this agenda. By instilling fear in the public and presenting climate change as an existential threat, governments and organizations can justify the implementation of policies that would otherwise be met with resistance. These policies often involve significant economic and social changes, such as carbon taxes, regulations on energy production, and restrictions on individual freedoms.

Furthermore, the false narrative of climate change allows for the exploitation of environmental concerns for political and financial gain. Many individuals and organizations have capitalized on the public's genuine desire to protect the environment by promoting green energy solutions and sustainable practices. However, behind these seemingly noble initiatives, there are often hidden agendas and ulterior motives.

One of the most glaring examples of this exploitation is the green energy industry. While renewable energy sources have their merits, they are often presented as the only solution to combat climate change. This narrow focus on green energy neglects other viable alternatives and fails to address the root causes of environmental degradation. Additionally, the green energy industry has become a lucrative business for those who have invested heavily in it, creating a conflict of interest that is rarely acknowledged.

Another aspect of the false narrative of climate change is the manipulation of data and scientific research. The scientific community is not immune to political and financial pressures, and there have been instances where data has been cherry-picked or manipulated to support a particular narrative. This manipulation undermines the integrity of scientific research and hinders our ability to accurately understand and address environmental issues.

It is important to note that questioning the false narrative of climate change does not mean denying the existence of environmental challenges or the need for sustainable practices. It simply means recognizing that there is more to the story than what is being presented to us. By critically examining the motivations behind the push for climate change policies, we can better understand the true agenda at play.

In conclusion, the false narrative of climate change serves as a powerful tool for those who seek to control and manipulate global affairs. By instilling fear and exploiting environmental concerns, governments and organizations can advance their agendas for global governance and population control. It is crucial that we question the mainstream narrative and seek a more comprehensive understanding of the complex issues at hand. Only then can we make informed decisions and work towards a truly sustainable and free world.

5.2 Green Energy Scams and Agenda 21

As we delve deeper into the sinister agenda of Agenda 21 and its successor, Agenda 2030, it becomes evident that the proponents of global genocide are not only focused on population control and economic warfare but also on exploiting environmental concerns. In this section, we will expose the green energy scams that are being used as a tool to further their agenda.

Under the guise of saving the planet and combating climate change, the proponents of Agenda 21 have pushed for the adoption of green energy solutions. While the idea of transitioning to renewable energy sources may seem noble and necessary, it is essential to understand the ulterior motives behind these initiatives.

One of the primary green energy scams is the promotion of unreliable and inefficient technologies such as wind and solar power. These technologies are heavily subsidized by governments and receive significant financial support from globalist organizations. However, despite the massive investments, they have proven to be inadequate in meeting the energy demands of modern societies.

The proponents of Agenda 21 use these green energy initiatives to create a false sense of progress and environmental responsibility. They manipulate public opinion by presenting these technologies as the solution to climate change and portray anyone who questions their effectiveness as climate change deniers or enemies of the planet. This tactic effectively silences dissent and prevents a critical examination of the true motives behind these initiatives.

Furthermore, the implementation of green energy solutions often leads to the destruction of natural habitats and landscapes. Large-scale wind and solar farms require vast amounts of land, which results in the displacement of wildlife and destruction of ecosystems. Additionally, the production and disposal of solar panels and wind turbines contribute to environmental pollution and waste.

Another aspect of the green energy scam is the promotion of carbon credits and carbon trading schemes. These mechanisms allow corporations and wealthy individuals to offset their carbon emissions by purchasing credits from projects that claim to reduce greenhouse gas emissions. However, these projects often have questionable environmental benefits and are primarily a means for the elite to maintain their polluting lifestyles while appearing environmentally conscious.

Agenda 21 also promotes the concept of "smart cities" as a solution to environmental challenges. These cities are presented as sustainable and technologically advanced, with integrated systems for energy management, transportation, and resource allocation. However, the reality is that smart cities are a means for increased surveillance and control over the population. The collection of vast amounts of data on individuals' behaviors and activities raises serious concerns about privacy and personal freedom.

It is crucial to recognize that the green energy scams promoted by Agenda 21 are not about saving the planet or creating a sustainable future. Instead, they serve as a means to consolidate power and control over resources. By promoting unreliable and inefficient technologies, the proponents of Agenda 21 ensure that societies remain dependent on centralized energy systems, allowing for greater manipulation and control.

To truly address environmental concerns, we must look beyond the green energy scams and focus on genuine solutions that prioritize innovation, efficiency, and individual freedom. This includes supporting research and development of advanced technologies, promoting decentralized energy production, and encouraging individual responsibility for sustainable practices.

In conclusion, the green energy scams promoted by Agenda 21 and Agenda 2030 are a means to further the global genocide agenda. By exploiting environmental concerns and manipulating public opinion, the proponents of these initiatives seek to consolidate power and control over resources. It is essential for individuals to educate themselves about the true motives behind these initiatives and advocate for genuine solutions that prioritize innovation, efficiency, and individual freedom. Only by exposing these scams can we hope to create a sustainable and free world for future generations.

5.3 Land Grabbing and Resource Control

One of the key strategies employed by the proponents of Agenda 21 and Agenda 2030 is the tactic of land grabbing and resource control. Under the guise of environmentalism and sustainable development, these globalist agendas seek to consolidate power and control over the world's natural resources, including land, water, minerals, and forests. This section will delve into the sinister motives behind this agenda and shed light on the devastating consequences it has for individual liberties and national sovereignty.

The Hidden Agenda

Land grabbing refers to the acquisition of large tracts of land, often by powerful corporations or governments, for various purposes such as industrial agriculture, mining, infrastructure development, or conservation. While these activities may seem innocuous on the surface, they are often driven by ulterior motives that serve the interests of the global elite. By controlling vast amounts of land and resources, these entities gain immense power and influence over nations and their populations.

Under the guise of sustainable development, Agenda 21 and Agenda 2030 promote the idea of land consolidation and resource control as a means to achieve their goals. They argue that centralized management of resources is necessary to ensure their equitable distribution and protect the environment. However, this narrative conveniently ignores the fact that such centralization inevitably leads to the concentration of power in the hands of a few, while eroding individual property rights and local autonomy.

Threats to Individual Liberties

Land grabbing and resource control pose significant threats to individual liberties and property rights. When governments or corporations seize control of land, they often displace local communities, depriving them of their homes, livelihoods, and cultural heritage. This not only violates basic human rights but also undermines the social fabric of communities and disrupts traditional ways of life.

Furthermore, the consolidation of land and resources in the hands of a few powerful entities leads to the marginalization of small-scale farmers, indigenous communities, and other vulnerable groups. These groups are often the most affected by land grabbing, as they rely on natural resources for their subsistence and have a deep connection to the land. By depriving them of their access to resources, Agenda 21 and Agenda 2030 perpetuate social inequality and exacerbate poverty and food insecurity.

Loss of National Sovereignty

Another alarming consequence of land grabbing and resource control is the erosion of national sovereignty. When powerful corporations or international organizations acquire control over a nation's resources, they effectively undermine the ability of that nation to make decisions in its own best interest. This loss of sovereignty is particularly concerning when it comes to vital resources such as water, which is essential for human survival and economic development.

By exerting control over water sources, for example, globalist entities can manipulate access to this precious resource, potentially leading to conflicts and geopolitical tensions. Moreover, the control of strategic resources by external actors undermines a nation's ability to pursue its own development agenda and hampers its economic independence.

Environmental Exploitation

Ironically, while Agenda 21 and Agenda 2030 claim to be driven by environmental concerns, the strategies they employ often result in the exploitation of natural resources rather than their preservation. Large-scale industrial agriculture, for instance, leads to deforestation, soil degradation, and the use of harmful chemicals, all of which have detrimental effects on ecosystems and biodiversity.

Similarly, mining activities driven by resource control often result in environmental degradation, including water pollution, habitat destruction, and the release of toxic substances into the environment. These activities not only harm the delicate balance of ecosystems but also threaten the livelihoods of local communities who depend on these resources for their survival.

Resisting Land Grabbing and Resource Control

To counter the insidious agenda of land grabbing and resource control, it is crucial for individuals, communities, and nations to assert their rights and protect their resources. This can be achieved through grassroots movements, legal challenges, and the promotion of sustainable and equitable resource management practices.

By raising awareness about the true motives behind Agenda 21 and Agenda 2030, individuals can resist the encroachment on their property rights and demand transparency and accountability from those in power. Additionally, fostering local self-reliance, supporting small-scale farmers, and promoting sustainable land and resource management practices can help counter the negative impacts of land grabbing and resource control.

In conclusion, land grabbing and resource control are integral components of the globalist agendas outlined in Agenda 21 and Agenda 2030. These strategies not only threaten individual liberties and national sovereignty but also exploit the environment and perpetuate social inequality. It is imperative for individuals and communities to stand up against these tactics and work towards a future that respects the rights of individuals, preserves the environment, and upholds the principles of freedom and sovereignty.

5.4 The Exploitation of Environmental Concerns

Environmental concerns have long been a topic of global importance. The health of our planet and the well-being of future generations depend on our ability to address these issues responsibly. However, what if I told you that there are those who seek to exploit these concerns for their own nefarious purposes? In this section, we will delve into the dark underbelly of the environmental movement and expose how it has been manipulated to further the agenda of global genocide.

One of the most insidious aspects of this exploitation is the use of fear tactics and misinformation. The proponents of Agenda 21 and Agenda 2030 have successfully created a false narrative of impending doom, convincing the masses that urgent action is needed to save the planet. By exaggerating the potential consequences of climate change and other environmental issues, they have instilled a sense of panic and urgency in the public, making it easier to manipulate and control them.

The exploitation of environmental concerns also extends to the promotion of green energy scams. While the idea of transitioning to renewable energy sources may seem noble, it has been hijacked by those with ulterior motives. The push for green energy has become a lucrative business for a select few, who profit off government subsidies and tax breaks while the average citizen bears the burden of higher energy costs. This not only perpetuates economic inequality but also diverts attention and resources away from more effective solutions to environmental problems.

Another aspect of this exploitation is the issue of land grabbing and resource control. Under the guise of environmental conservation, powerful entities have been able to seize control of vast tracts of land and resources, displacing indigenous communities and undermining local autonomy. This not only violates the rights of these communities but also consolidates power in the hands of a few, furthering the agenda of global governance and control.

It is important to recognize that the exploitation of environmental concerns is not limited to the economic and political realms. The psychological manipulation of the masses plays a crucial role in advancing this agenda. Through the use of propaganda and brainwashing techniques, the public is conditioned to accept and support policies that are detrimental to their own well-being. Dissent and critical thinking are suppressed, and those who dare to question the official narrative are labeled as conspiracy theorists or deniers.

Furthermore, the exploitation of environmental concerns extends to the silencing of truth seekers. Whistleblowers and individuals who dare to expose the truth behind Agenda 21 and Agenda 2030 are often marginalized, discredited, or even threatened. Their voices are drowned out by the mainstream media, which serves as a mouthpiece for the globalist agenda. This suppression of dissent ensures that the masses remain ignorant and compliant, allowing the agenda of global genocide to proceed unchecked.

The exploitation of environmental concerns is a multi-faceted strategy employed by the global elite to further their agenda of control and domination. By manipulating public sentiment, diverting resources, and suppressing dissent, they are able to advance their goals without arousing suspicion. It is imperative that we remain vigilant and informed, questioning the narratives presented to us and seeking the truth behind the facade.

In conclusion, the exploitation of environmental concerns is a disturbing reality that must be exposed. The manipulation of fear, the promotion of green energy scams, the land grabbing and resource control, the psychological manipulation, and the silencing of truth seekers are all tactics employed to further the agenda of global genocide. It is up to us, the citizens of the world, to resist this exploitation and fight for a future that is truly sustainable and free.

Education and Indoctrination

6.1 Reprogramming the Youth

One of the most insidious aspects of Agenda 21 and Agenda 2030 is the deliberate targeting of the youth. The globalists behind these agendas understand that in order to fully implement their plans for global genocide, they must first reprogram the minds of the next generation. By controlling education systems and indoctrinating young minds, they can mold a generation of compliant citizens who will unknowingly support and perpetuate their destructive agenda.

The reprogramming of the youth begins in schools, where children are subjected to a carefully crafted curriculum designed to promote globalist ideals and suppress critical thinking. Common Core, a globalist-driven educational initiative, plays a significant role in this process. Under the guise of improving education standards, Common Core actually serves as a tool for indoctrination. It promotes conformity, discourages independent thought, and stifles creativity.

Globalist curriculum infiltrates every subject, from history to science, and presents a distorted view of the world. It emphasizes the importance of global governance and downplays the significance of national sovereignty. Children are taught to prioritize the needs of the collective over individual liberties, and to view themselves as global citizens rather than citizens of their respective countries. This indoctrination erodes the sense of national identity and fosters a sense of dependency on global institutions.

Critical thinking is actively discouraged in these educational systems. Students are discouraged from questioning the official narrative and are instead taught to accept information at face value. This suppression of critical thinking is a deliberate tactic employed by the globalists to ensure that the youth do not question the validity of Agenda 21 and Agenda 2030. By discouraging independent thought, the globalists can maintain control over the narrative and prevent any dissenting voices from emerging.

The goal of this reprogramming is to create a generation of compliant citizens who will willingly accept the globalist agenda without question. These young individuals will be more susceptible to propaganda and misinformation, making them ideal targets for manipulation. By controlling the education system, the globalists can shape the beliefs and values of the youth, ensuring their continued support for the agenda of global genocide.

Furthermore, the reprogramming of the youth extends beyond the classroom. The media plays a crucial role in this process, bombarding young minds with propaganda and misinformation. Television shows, movies, and social media platforms are all used as tools to shape the beliefs and values of the youth. Through these mediums, the globalists can further reinforce their narrative and manipulate the perceptions of the younger generation.

The consequences of this reprogramming are far-reaching. A generation of individuals who have been indoctrinated from a young age will be more likely to support policies that align with the globalist agenda. They will be less likely to question the erosion of individual liberties and the rise of global governance. This reprogramming creates a fertile ground for the globalists to implement their plans for global genocide, as the youth will unknowingly contribute to the destruction of their own future.

However, there is hope. The power of awareness and critical thinking cannot be underestimated. By exposing the reprogramming of the youth and educating others about the true intentions behind Agenda 21 and Agenda 2030, we can begin to counteract the effects of this indoctrination. It is crucial that we encourage independent thought and foster a spirit of questioning among the youth. By empowering them with knowledge and encouraging them to think critically, we can help them resist the manipulation and become active participants in shaping a better future.

In conclusion, the reprogramming of the youth is a key component of the globalist agenda for global genocide. By controlling education systems and manipulating the media, the globalists aim to mold a generation of compliant citizens who will unknowingly support their destructive plans. However, through awareness and critical thinking, we can empower the youth to resist this indoctrination and become agents of change. It is imperative that we take a stand against the reprogramming of the youth and work towards creating a future that prioritizes individual liberties and safeguards the well-being of humanity.

6.2 Common Core and Globalist Curriculum

Education is a powerful tool that can shape the minds of future generations. It is through education that ideas, values, and beliefs are instilled in young minds, ultimately influencing their perspectives and actions. However, when education becomes a means of indoctrination rather than enlightenment, it becomes a dangerous weapon in the hands of those with ulterior motives. In the context of Agenda 21 and Agenda 2030, the globalist agenda extends its reach into the realm of education through initiatives such as Common Core and the implementation of a globalist curriculum.

The Origins of Common Core

Common Core is an educational initiative that was introduced in the United States in 2010. It was marketed as a set of standards aimed at improving the quality of education and ensuring that students are prepared for college and the workforce. However, beneath the surface, Common Core has been criticized for its centralization of education and its alignment with the globalist agenda.

The development of Common Core was heavily influenced by organizations such as the National Governors Association (NGA) and the Council of Chief State School Officers (CCSSO). These organizations, funded by powerful globalist entities, played a significant role in shaping the curriculum and standards. The involvement of these organizations raises questions about the true intentions behind Common Core and its alignment with the globalist agenda.

The Globalist Curriculum

One of the key concerns surrounding Common Core is the content of the curriculum itself. Critics argue that the curriculum promotes a globalist worldview, emphasizing concepts such as global citizenship, sustainability, and social justice. While these may seem like noble ideals on the surface, they are often used as a means to push a specific agenda and suppress alternative viewpoints.

The globalist curriculum seeks to mold students into compliant citizens who unquestioningly accept the narratives and values promoted by the globalist elite. It discourages critical thinking and independent thought, instead promoting conformity and adherence to the globalist agenda. By controlling the education system, the globalists can shape the beliefs and values of future generations, ensuring their continued dominance and control.

Indoctrination and Suppression of Critical Thinking

One of the most concerning aspects of the globalist curriculum is its emphasis on indoctrination rather than education. Students are often taught what to think rather than how to think critically. Alternative viewpoints and dissenting opinions are often suppressed or labeled as "conspiracy theories," discouraging students from questioning the official narratives.

Critical thinking is a fundamental skill that allows individuals to analyze information, evaluate evidence, and form independent opinions. By suppressing critical thinking, the globalist curriculum effectively stifles intellectual curiosity and promotes a culture of conformity. This not only hinders the development of well-rounded individuals but also undermines the principles of democracy and free thought.

Creating Compliant Citizens

The ultimate goal of the globalist curriculum is to create a generation of compliant citizens who are easily manipulated and controlled. By shaping the beliefs and values of young minds, the globalists can ensure that their agenda is perpetuated and their power remains unchallenged. Through the education system, they can mold individuals who are loyal to the globalist cause and who will actively work towards its realization.

The globalist curriculum also promotes a sense of global citizenship, eroding national identities and fostering a sense of allegiance to a global authority. This further serves the globalist agenda of eroding national sovereignty and establishing a centralized global governance system. By instilling a globalist worldview in students, the education system becomes a powerful tool for advancing the globalist agenda.

In conclusion, the implementation of Common Core and the globalist curriculum is a concerning development in the context of Agenda 21 and Agenda 2030. Education, which should be a means of enlightenment and empowerment, is being used as a tool for indoctrination and control. By shaping the beliefs and values of young minds, the globalist elite can ensure the perpetuation of their agenda and the realization of their vision for a globalist world. It is crucial for individuals to be aware of these manipulations and to actively resist the indoctrination that is taking place in our education systems. Only through critical thinking and a commitment to preserving individual liberties can we hope to overcome the globalist agenda and create a future that is truly free and sustainable.

6.3 The Suppression of Critical Thinking

One of the most insidious aspects of Agenda 21 and Agenda 2030 is the deliberate suppression of critical thinking. The architects of these global plans understand that an informed and critically thinking population poses a significant threat to their agenda. Therefore, they have implemented various strategies to stifle independent thought and ensure compliance with their narrative.

Indoctrination in Education

One of the primary methods used to suppress critical thinking is through the education system. From an early age, children are subjected to a curriculum that promotes conformity and discourages questioning. The focus is on rote memorization and regurgitation of information rather than fostering analytical skills and independent thought.

Under the guise of "global citizenship" and "sustainability," students are taught a one-sided view of the world that aligns with the goals of Agenda 21 and Agenda 2030. Dissenting opinions or alternative perspectives are often dismissed or labeled as conspiracy theories, effectively shutting down any critical examination of the issues at hand.

Common Core and Globalist Curriculum

The implementation of Common Core standards in many countries has further contributed to the suppression of critical thinking. These standards prioritize conformity and standardized testing over genuine intellectual inquiry. The emphasis on memorization and regurgitation of information leaves little room for students to develop their own thoughts and ideas.

Furthermore, the curriculum itself is often designed to promote a globalist agenda. History is rewritten, facts are distorted, and critical events are omitted or downplayed to fit a predetermined narrative. This indoctrination ensures that future generations are unaware of the true intentions behind Agenda 21 and Agenda 2030, making them more susceptible to manipulation and control.

Censorship and Media Manipulation

Another powerful tool used to suppress critical thinking is censorship and media manipulation. The mainstream media, which is largely controlled by a handful of globalist corporations, plays a crucial role in shaping public opinion and controlling the narrative. Dissenting voices and alternative viewpoints are marginalized or completely silenced, while propaganda and misinformation are disseminated on a massive scale.

Through carefully crafted narratives and emotional manipulation, the media creates a false sense of consensus and discourages independent thought. Those who dare to question the official narrative are often labeled as extremists or conspiracy theorists, effectively discrediting their arguments and discouraging others from engaging in critical analysis.

Social Conditioning and Peer Pressure

Social conditioning and peer pressure also play a significant role in suppressing critical thinking. Society has become increasingly polarized, with individuals who hold dissenting views being ostracized and ridiculed. This creates a climate of fear and conformity, where individuals are hesitant to express their true thoughts and opinions for fear of social backlash.

Additionally, the rise of social media has further exacerbated this issue. Algorithms and echo chambers ensure that individuals are exposed only to information that aligns with their existing beliefs, reinforcing confirmation bias and discouraging critical examination of opposing viewpoints.

Overcoming the Suppression

Despite the concerted efforts to suppress critical thinking, there is still hope. It is crucial for individuals to actively seek out diverse perspectives, question the information presented to them, and engage in independent research. Developing strong analytical skills and the ability to think critically is essential in navigating the complex web of deception surrounding Agenda 21 and Agenda 2030.

Furthermore, it is important to foster an environment that encourages open dialogue and respectful debate. By creating spaces where individuals feel safe to express their thoughts and challenge prevailing narratives, we can begin to break free from the chains of suppression and reclaim our ability to think critically.

In conclusion, the suppression of critical thinking is a deliberate tactic employed by the architects of Agenda 21 and Agenda 2030 to ensure compliance with their globalist agenda. Through indoctrination in education, media manipulation, censorship, and social conditioning, they seek to create a population that unquestioningly accepts their narrative. However, by actively engaging in critical thinking and promoting open dialogue, we can begin to dismantle the walls of suppression and reclaim our intellectual freedom.

6.4 Creating a Generation of Compliant Citizens

One of the most insidious aspects of Agenda 21 and Agenda 2030 is the deliberate effort to create a generation of compliant citizens. Through various means of indoctrination and manipulation, the architects of this global genocide plan aim to mold individuals who will unquestioningly follow their agenda and willingly surrender their freedoms.

Education plays a crucial role in this process. The reprogramming of the youth is a key strategy employed by those behind Agenda 21. Section 6.1 of this book has already explored this topic in detail, highlighting how the curriculum is designed to shape young minds into accepting the principles and goals of the globalist agenda. However, the manipulation doesn't stop there.

Under the guise of promoting critical thinking and global citizenship, the architects of Agenda 21 have implemented programs such as Common Core and a globalist curriculum. Section 6.2 delves into the specifics of these initiatives, exposing how they are used to indoctrinate students with a particular worldview that aligns with the goals of the global elite. By controlling the information and narratives presented in schools, they can shape the beliefs and values of future generations.

Critical thinking is a threat to the agenda, and therefore, it must be suppressed. Section 6.3 of this book explores how the education system actively discourages independent thought and skepticism. Students are discouraged from questioning authority or challenging the official narratives. Instead, they are taught to accept information at face value and regurgitate it without question. This creates a generation of compliant citizens who are easily manipulated and controlled.

But how exactly do they ensure compliance? Section 6.4 uncovers the methods employed to create a generation of individuals who will willingly follow the globalist agenda. One of the most effective strategies is the suppression of individuality and the promotion of conformity. By discouraging independent thought and encouraging groupthink, the architects of Agenda 21 can mold individuals who are more likely to conform to their desired outcomes.

The education system also plays a role in promoting conformity. Students are taught to value consensus over dissent, and those who deviate from the accepted norms are often ostracized or labeled as troublemakers. This creates a culture of conformity, where individuals are afraid to speak out or question the status quo. As a result, dissenting voices are silenced, and the globalist agenda can proceed unchallenged.

Another method used to create compliant citizens is the manipulation of emotions and the promotion of fear. Section 6.4 explores how fear is used as a tool to control and manipulate individuals. By instilling a sense of impending doom and catastrophe, the architects of Agenda 21 can create a sense of urgency and desperation. In this state of fear, individuals are more likely to accept drastic measures and surrender their freedoms in the name of security.

Furthermore, the education system is used to promote a sense of dependency on authority figures. Students are taught to rely on experts and government institutions for guidance and solutions. This fosters a mindset of reliance on external authorities, making individuals more susceptible to manipulation and control.

Creating a generation of compliant citizens also involves the suppression of dissenting voices and the marginalization of truth seekers. Section 6.4 exposes how those who dare to question the globalist agenda are often labeled as conspiracy theorists or extremists. Their views are dismissed and ridiculed, effectively silencing any opposition. By controlling the narrative and marginalizing dissent, the architects of Agenda 21 can maintain their grip on power and ensure the compliance of the masses.

In conclusion, the architects of Agenda 21 and Agenda 2030 are actively working to create a generation of compliant citizens who will unquestioningly follow their globalist agenda. Through the manipulation of education, suppression of critical thinking, promotion of conformity, and instilling fear and dependency, they aim to mold individuals who will willingly surrender their freedoms and accept the global genocide plan. It is crucial for individuals to recognize these tactics and resist the indoctrination, for only through awareness and unity can we overcome this evil agenda and preserve our individual liberties and sovereignty.

Healthcare and Population Control

7.1 The Pharmaceutical Industry's Role

The pharmaceutical industry plays a significant role in the agenda of global genocide outlined in Agenda 21 and Agenda 2030. While many people trust pharmaceutical companies to provide them with safe and effective medications, there is a dark side to this industry that is often overlooked. In this section, we will explore the ways in which the pharmaceutical industry contributes to population control and the manipulation of healthcare systems.

One of the key ways in which the pharmaceutical industry contributes to global genocide is through the production and distribution of harmful medications. It is no secret that many pharmaceutical drugs come with a long list of potential side effects, some of which can be severe or even life-threatening. These side effects are often downplayed or hidden from the public, allowing these companies to profit while putting people's lives at risk.

In addition to the direct harm caused by certain medications, the pharmaceutical industry also plays a role in promoting a culture of dependency on drugs. Rather than focusing on preventative measures or natural remedies, pharmaceutical companies often push for the use of their products as the primary solution to health issues. This not only leads to overmedication but also perpetuates a cycle of reliance on pharmaceutical interventions, further enriching these companies at the expense of public health.

Furthermore, the pharmaceutical industry has been known to engage in unethical practices such as off-label marketing and the suppression of negative research findings. Off-label marketing refers to the promotion of a drug for uses that have not been approved by regulatory authorities. This allows pharmaceutical companies to expand their market and increase profits, even if it means putting patients at risk. Additionally, the suppression of negative research findings prevents the public from being fully informed about the potential risks and benefits of certain medications.

Another concerning aspect of the pharmaceutical industry's role in global genocide is its involvement in the development and distribution of vaccines. While vaccines have undoubtedly played a crucial role in preventing the spread of infectious diseases, there are legitimate concerns about the safety and efficacy of certain vaccines. The push for mandatory vaccination programs without proper informed consent raises questions about individual rights and the potential for coercion.

Furthermore, there have been allegations that certain vaccines may be used as a covert method of population control. While these claims are often dismissed as conspiracy theories, it is essential to critically examine the evidence and consider the potential motives behind such actions. The use of vaccines to control fertility or manipulate the immune system is not entirely far-fetched, given the history of unethical medical experiments and the pursuit of population control agendas.

Reproductive rights and eugenics also come into play when discussing the pharmaceutical industry's role in global genocide. There have been instances where pharmaceutical companies have been involved in the development and promotion of contraceptives that have had devastating effects on certain populations. The targeting of specific ethnic or socio-economic groups with the intention of reducing their fertility rates raises serious ethical concerns and highlights the potential for the pharmaceutical industry to be complicit in population control efforts.

Controlling healthcare access and quality is another way in which the pharmaceutical industry contributes to global genocide. By monopolizing the market and driving up the prices of essential medications, pharmaceutical companies create barriers to healthcare for many individuals, particularly those in low-income communities. This lack of access to affordable and necessary treatments can have severe consequences, leading to increased morbidity and mortality rates.

In conclusion, the pharmaceutical industry's role in global genocide cannot be ignored. From the production and distribution of harmful medications to the promotion of a culture of dependency on drugs, this industry has a significant impact on public health. The involvement in the development and distribution of vaccines, as well as the potential for covert population control, raises serious ethical concerns. It is crucial for individuals to be aware of these issues and advocate for transparency, accountability, and the prioritization of public health over corporate profits.

7.2 Vaccines and Depopulation Agenda

Vaccines have long been hailed as one of the greatest achievements in modern medicine. They have played a crucial role in eradicating deadly diseases and saving countless lives. However, what if I told you that vaccines are not always what they seem? What if I told you that they could be used as a tool for population control and even depopulation? In this section, we will delve into the dark side of vaccines and expose the hidden agenda behind their use.

Before we proceed, it is important to clarify that not all vaccines are part of a depopulation agenda. The majority of vaccines are safe and effective, designed to protect individuals from harmful diseases. However, there is evidence to suggest that certain vaccines may be used for purposes beyond their intended benefits.

One of the key concerns surrounding vaccines and depopulation is the use of sterilizing agents. It has been alleged that some vaccines contain substances that can impair fertility or cause infertility in individuals. This raises serious ethical questions about the true intentions behind these vaccines. Are they truly meant to protect public health, or are they being used to control population growth?

Another aspect of the depopulation agenda is the potential use of vaccines to spread diseases rather than prevent them. This may sound counterintuitive, but it is a strategy that has been theorized by some researchers. The idea is that certain vaccines could be engineered to contain live viruses or other pathogens that could infect individuals and spread throughout the population. This would result in a controlled reduction in population size.

While these claims may seem far-fetched, it is important to consider the historical context in which they arise. Throughout history, there have been instances where governments and organizations have used medical interventions for nefarious purposes. The Tuskegee syphilis experiment, for example, involved withholding treatment from African American men to study the progression of the disease. This serves as a reminder that we must remain vigilant and question the motives behind medical interventions, including vaccines.

It is also worth noting that the depopulation agenda is often linked to concerns about overpopulation and limited resources. Proponents of this agenda argue that reducing the global population is necessary to ensure the sustainability of the planet. However, the methods proposed to achieve this goal, such as using vaccines for population control, raise serious ethical and human rights concerns.

It is crucial to approach these claims with skepticism and demand transparency from those responsible for vaccine development and distribution. Independent research and rigorous scientific studies are essential to verify the safety and efficacy of vaccines. Additionally, whistleblowers play a vital role in exposing any potential wrongdoing or hidden agendas.

It is important to emphasize that the majority of vaccines are safe and have been proven to save lives. Vaccination programs have successfully eradicated diseases such as smallpox and polio, leading to significant improvements in global public health. However, we must remain vigilant and ensure that vaccines are not being misused or manipulated for ulterior motives.

In conclusion, while vaccines have undoubtedly played a crucial role in protecting public health, it is essential to remain critical and question the motives behind their development and use. The potential for vaccines to be used as a tool for population control or depopulation should not be dismissed outright. Vigilance, transparency, and independent research are key to ensuring the safety and integrity of vaccination programs. As responsible citizens, we must continue to demand accountability and protect our fundamental rights to health and well-being.

7.3 Reproductive Rights and Eugenics

Reproductive rights and eugenics are two interconnected aspects of the global genocide plan outlined in Agenda 21 and Agenda 2030. These agendas aim to control and manipulate the world's population through various means, including the restriction of reproductive rights and the implementation of eugenic practices. In this section, we will delve into the sinister strategies employed by the global elite to achieve their goals.

The Attack on Reproductive Rights

One of the most effective ways to control population growth is by limiting individuals' reproductive rights. Under the guise of promoting women's health and empowerment, the global elite have pushed for policies and initiatives that restrict access to contraception, family planning, and abortion services. By controlling these aspects of reproductive health, they can manipulate population growth and ensure their desired outcomes.

These policies are often disguised as efforts to protect the environment or promote sustainable development. However, upon closer examination, it becomes clear that their true purpose is to exert control over individuals' reproductive choices. By limiting access to contraception and family planning, the global elite can effectively dictate who can have children and when, thereby manipulating population numbers to align with their agenda.

Eugenics: The Dark Side of Population Control

Eugenics, the study of or belief in the possibility of improving the qualities of the human species or a human population, especially by such means as discouraging reproduction by persons having genetic defects or presumed to have inheritable undesirable traits (negative eugenics) or encouraging reproduction by persons presumed to have inheritable desirable traits (positive eugenics).

Eugenics has a dark and troubling history, with its roots dating back to the early 20th century. It gained popularity among certain groups who believed in the superiority of certain races or genetic traits. These proponents of eugenics sought to eliminate what they considered "undesirable" traits from the gene pool through forced sterilization, segregation, and even euthanasia.

While eugenics fell out of favor after the atrocities committed during World War II, it has resurfaced in a more subtle form within the framework of Agenda 21 and Agenda 2030. The global elite, under the guise of promoting sustainability and population control, are implementing policies and practices that effectively amount to eugenics.

Covert Measures and Coercion

The global elite employ various covert measures and coercion tactics to enforce their reproductive control agenda. These include:

1. **Forced Sterilization:** In some parts of the world, particularly in developing countries, forced sterilization programs have been implemented under the guise of providing healthcare services. Vulnerable populations, such as women from marginalized communities, are often targeted and subjected to sterilization without their informed consent.
2. **Population Control Incentives:** In certain countries, the global elite offer financial incentives to individuals who agree to limit their family size or undergo sterilization. While these incentives may appear attractive on the surface, they are designed to manipulate individuals into making reproductive choices that align with the global elite's agenda.
3. **Biased Family Planning Programs:** Family planning programs funded by international organizations often prioritize certain methods of contraception over others. This bias can limit individuals' choices

and force them into using methods that may not be suitable for their health or personal preferences.

4. **Selective Access to Healthcare:** The global elite also manipulate access to healthcare services, particularly reproductive healthcare, to control population growth. By limiting access to contraception, prenatal care, and safe abortion services, they can effectively control the reproductive choices of individuals and communities.

The Ethical Dilemma

The restriction of reproductive rights and the implementation of eugenic practices raise significant ethical concerns. Every individual has the right to make informed decisions about their reproductive health and family planning. By infringing upon these rights, the global elite are not only violating basic human rights but also perpetuating a system of control and manipulation.

Furthermore, the implementation of eugenic practices based on subjective judgments of genetic desirability is deeply problematic. It reinforces discriminatory beliefs and perpetuates social inequalities. It is essential to recognize that every individual has inherent worth and should not be subjected to judgment or control based on their genetic makeup.

The Fight for Reproductive Freedom

To combat the global elite's assault on reproductive rights and eugenic practices, it is crucial to raise awareness and advocate for reproductive freedom. This includes:

1. **Education and Awareness:** Spreading knowledge about the true intentions behind population control measures is essential. By educating individuals about their reproductive rights and the potential consequences of restrictive policies, we can empower them to make informed choices and resist manipulation.

2. **Advocacy and Activism:** Supporting organizations and movements that fight for reproductive rights is crucial. By joining forces with

like-minded individuals and advocating for policies that protect reproductive freedom, we can challenge the global elite's agenda and ensure that every individual has the right to make decisions about their own bodies and families.

3. **Legal Challenges:** Challenging restrictive reproductive policies through legal means can be an effective strategy. By working with legal experts and human rights organizations, we can challenge laws and regulations that infringe upon reproductive rights and hold the global elite accountable for their actions.

4. **Promoting Inclusive and Comprehensive Reproductive Healthcare:** Ensuring access to comprehensive reproductive healthcare services, including contraception, family planning, and safe abortion, is essential. By promoting inclusive and non-discriminatory healthcare systems, we can protect individuals' rights and provide them with the resources they need to make informed choices.

In conclusion, reproductive rights and eugenics are integral components of the global genocide plan outlined in Agenda 21 and Agenda 2030. By restricting reproductive rights and implementing eugenic practices, the global elite seek to control and manipulate the world's population. It is crucial to recognize and resist these tactics, advocating for reproductive freedom and ensuring that every individual has the right to make decisions about their own bodies and families.

7.4 Controlling Healthcare Access and Quality

One of the most insidious aspects of the Agenda 21 and Agenda 2030 plans is the control over healthcare access and quality. Under the guise of promoting sustainable development and improving global health, the architects of these agendas have devised a system that allows them to manipulate and restrict healthcare services to further their goals of population control.

The Weaponization of Healthcare

Healthcare is a fundamental human right, and it should be accessible to all individuals regardless of their socioeconomic status or geographical location. However, the proponents of Agenda 21 and Agenda 2030 have perverted this noble concept and turned it into a tool for control and manipulation.

By controlling healthcare access, the global elite can effectively dictate who receives medical treatment and who does not. This allows them to selectively target certain populations for depopulation while ensuring the survival and well-being of those they deem worthy. It is a chilling and dystopian vision of a world where the value of human life is determined by a select few.

Restricting Access to Healthcare

One of the ways in which healthcare access is controlled is through the implementation of policies that limit the availability of medical services. This can be achieved through various means, such as the establishment of healthcare monopolies, the rationing of resources, and the imposition of strict regulations and licensing requirements.

By consolidating control over healthcare providers and facilities, the global elite can effectively limit the number of healthcare options available to the general population. This not only restricts access to medical treatment but also allows them to dictate the quality of care provided. In this way, they can ensure that only those who align with their agenda receive the best healthcare services, while the rest are left to suffer.

Manipulating Healthcare Quality

Controlling healthcare quality is another tactic employed by the proponents of Agenda 21 and Agenda 2030. By setting standards and guidelines for medical practice, they can dictate the type of treatments and interventions that are deemed acceptable. This allows them to suppress alternative and holistic approaches to healthcare that may challenge their narrative.

Furthermore, the global elite can manipulate healthcare quality by influencing medical education and research. By funding and promoting certain studies and suppressing others, they can shape the medical knowledge and practices that are taught to healthcare professionals. This ensures that the next generation of doctors and nurses are indoctrinated into their agenda and are less likely to question or deviate from the established norms.

The Impact on Global Health

The consequences of controlling healthcare access and quality are far-reaching and devastating. By restricting access to medical treatment, countless lives are lost unnecessarily. Those who are denied healthcare services due to their socioeconomic status or geographical location suffer needlessly, while the global elite continue to thrive.

Moreover, by manipulating healthcare quality, the global elite can perpetuate a system that prioritizes profit over patient well-being. Pharmaceutical companies, for example, can push for the use of expensive and potentially harmful drugs, while suppressing safer and more affordable alternatives. This not only leads to unnecessary suffering but also perpetuates a cycle of dependency on the healthcare system.

The Fight for Healthcare Freedom

It is crucial for individuals to recognize the importance of healthcare freedom and to resist the control and manipulation imposed by the proponents of Agenda 21 and Agenda 2030. By advocating for universal access to healthcare and demanding transparency and accountability from healthcare providers and policymakers, we can begin to dismantle the system of control that has been put in place.

Additionally, supporting alternative and holistic approaches to healthcare can help to break free from the narrow confines of the mainstream medical establishment. By embracing a more comprehensive and patient-centered approach, we can empower individuals to take control of their own health and well-being.

In conclusion, the control over healthcare access and quality is a key component of the Agenda 21 and Agenda 2030 plans. By manipulating healthcare services, the global elite can further their goals of population control and ensure their own survival and dominance. It is imperative that we recognize and resist this insidious agenda, advocating for healthcare freedom and the right of every individual to receive quality medical treatment. Only through unity and awareness can we hope to overcome the forces that seek to control and manipulate our healthcare systems.

Resistance and Awakening

8.1 The Power of Awareness

In the battle against global genocide, one of the most powerful weapons we have is awareness. The power to expose the truth behind Agenda 21 and Agenda 2030 lies in our ability to educate ourselves and others about the sinister plans that have been set in motion. By shedding light on the dark corners of this agenda, we can begin to dismantle the machinery of destruction and work towards a better future for humanity.

The first step in harnessing the power of awareness is understanding the true nature of Agenda 21 and Agenda 2030. These global initiatives, disguised as sustainable development plans, are in fact a blueprint for control and depopulation. They were drafted by a group of individuals who saw themselves as the architects of a new world order, where the masses would be manipulated and controlled for the benefit of a select few.

It is crucial to expose the names of those who drafted these agendas, as they are the masterminds behind the global genocide plan. By bringing their identities to light, we can hold them accountable for their actions and ensure that their plans do not go unnoticed or unchallenged. These individuals, hidden in the shadows, must be exposed for the world to see.

Equally important is unveiling the endorsers and promoters of Agenda 21 and Agenda 2030. These are the individuals, organizations, and governments that have willingly aligned themselves with the agenda, either out of ignorance or a desire for power and control. By exposing their involvement, we can raise awareness about the extent of the support for this genocidal plan and encourage others to question their allegiance.

To truly understand the depth of the global genocide plan, we must delve into the tactics employed by the deep state. This shadowy network of individuals and organizations operates behind the scenes, manipulating governments, economies, and societies to further their agenda. By understanding their methods, we can begin to dismantle their control and reclaim our freedom.

One of the key methods employed by the deep state is population control. Through various means such as forced sterilizations, mass vaccinations, and the promotion of abortion, they seek to reduce the global population to a more manageable level. By exposing these methods, we can empower individuals to make informed decisions about their own reproductive health and challenge the narrative that population control is necessary for a sustainable future.

The numbers game is another tool used by the deep state to further their agenda. By manipulating statistics and creating false narratives, they aim to instill fear and compliance in the masses. It is crucial to expose the truth behind these numbers and question the motives behind the alarming predictions of overpopulation and environmental catastrophe. Only through critical thinking and independent research can we uncover the truth and challenge the false narratives.

Documented facts and evidence play a crucial role in exposing the global genocide plan. By compiling and presenting irrefutable evidence, we can dismantle the web of lies and propaganda that has been woven around Agenda 21 and Agenda 2030. From leaked documents to insider testimonies, every piece of evidence adds to the puzzle and strengthens our case against those perpetrating this evil agenda.

In the fight against global genocide, awareness is our most powerful weapon. By understanding the true nature of Agenda 21 and Agenda 2030, exposing the names of those involved, and presenting the documented facts and evidence, we can awaken others to the reality of this genocidal plan. Together, we can build a united front against the forces of destruction and work towards a future where freedom, truth, and justice prevail.

8.2 Exposing the Agenda

In this section, we will delve deeper into the sinister agenda behind Agenda 21 and Agenda 2030. We will expose the individuals and organizations responsible for drafting and endorsing these plans, as well as shed light on the methods and numbers involved in their pursuit of global genocide. Through documented facts and evidence, we will uncover the truth that has been hidden from the public for far too long.

The Drafters of Agenda 21

Agenda 21 was first introduced at the United Nations Conference on Environment and Development in Rio de Janeiro in 1992. While it may seem like a well-intentioned plan for sustainable development, the truth is far more sinister. The drafters of Agenda 21, including Maurice Strong, a Canadian businessman and UN bureaucrat, had a hidden agenda. They sought to consolidate power and control over nations and individuals under the guise of environmentalism.

Maurice Strong, along with other influential figures such as Gro Harlem Brundtland, the former Prime Minister of Norway, and Mikhail Gorbachev, the former President of the Soviet Union, played key roles in shaping the agenda. These individuals, driven by their own ideological beliefs and desire for global governance, crafted a plan that would ultimately lead to the destruction of national sovereignty and individual freedoms.

The Endorsers and Promoters

Agenda 21 and its successor, Agenda 2030, have gained widespread support and endorsement from various governments, non-governmental organizations (NGOs), and influential individuals. These endorsers and promoters include politicians, environmental activists, and even celebrities who have been misled into believing that these agendas are for the betterment of humanity.

One of the most prominent endorsers of Agenda 21 is the United Nations itself. Through its various agencies and programs, the UN has been actively promoting and implementing the agenda worldwide. Additionally, many governments, particularly those with a globalist agenda, have embraced and incorporated the principles of Agenda 21 into their policies and legislation.

NGOs such as the Sierra Club, Greenpeace, and the World Wildlife Fund have also played a significant role in promoting the agenda. These organizations, often funded by powerful elites and corporate interests, have used their influence to push for the implementation of Agenda 21, furthering the globalist agenda and consolidating power in the hands of a few.

The Deep State's Agenda

Behind the seemingly noble goals of sustainable development and environmental protection lies a hidden agenda of the deep state. The deep state, a shadowy network of unelected bureaucrats, corporate interests, and influential individuals, seeks to exert control over nations and populations for their own gain.

Their methods of control are multifaceted and insidious. They include economic warfare, manipulation of financial systems, and the destruction of national economies. By creating financial dependency and instability, the deep state can effectively control governments and manipulate policies to further their globalist agenda.

Methods of Population Control

One of the most alarming aspects of Agenda 21 and Agenda 2030 is the methods of population control employed by the deep state. These methods include forced sterilization, mass vaccination campaigns, and the promotion of reproductive rights and eugenics.

Under the guise of healthcare and reproductive rights, the deep state seeks to control and manipulate the population. Through the use of vaccines, they can introduce harmful substances into individuals, leading to long-term health issues and even infertility. Additionally, the promotion of reproductive rights and eugenics allows them to selectively control who can reproduce, furthering their agenda of population control.

The Numbers Game

To achieve their goals of global genocide, the deep state has set specific targets and numbers. These targets include reducing the global population to a more manageable level, as they believe that overpopulation is the root cause of many of the world's problems.

While the exact numbers and targets are not publicly disclosed, it is clear that the deep state aims to drastically reduce the world's population through various means. This includes controlling access to healthcare, promoting harmful environmental policies, and manipulating economic systems to create poverty and dependency.

Documented Facts and Evidence

The evidence exposing the true agenda behind Agenda 21 and Agenda 2030 is extensive and well-documented. Numerous research studies, reports, and testimonies from whistleblowers have shed light on the hidden motives and methods employed by the deep state.

These documents and accounts provide undeniable proof of the global genocide plan and the individuals and organizations involved. They serve as a wake-up call to citizens of the world, urging them to take action and resist the implementation of these destructive agendas.

In the next section, we will explore the role of propaganda and misinformation in furthering the deep state's agenda, as well as the media's complicity in spreading their narrative. We will uncover the tactics used to brainwash the masses and silence truth seekers, and discuss strategies for building alliances and networks to resist global genocide.

8.3 Building Alliances and Networks

In the fight against the global genocide agenda of Agenda 21 and Agenda 2030, it is crucial for concerned citizens to come together and build alliances and networks. The power of unity and collective action cannot be underestimated when it comes to exposing the truth and resisting the forces behind these destructive plans. By joining forces, we can amplify our voices, share information, and work towards a common goal of preserving individual liberties and protecting humanity.

The Importance of Collaboration

Building alliances and networks is essential for several reasons. Firstly, it allows for the pooling of resources, knowledge, and expertise. Each individual or organization brings unique skills and perspectives to the table, and by collaborating, we can leverage these strengths to create a more impactful movement. Together, we can conduct research, gather evidence, and expose the truth in a comprehensive and coordinated manner.

Secondly, alliances and networks provide a support system for those who are actively resisting the global genocide agenda. It can be a lonely and challenging journey to go against powerful forces, but knowing that there are others who share the same concerns and are fighting alongside can provide encouragement and motivation. Through these networks, individuals can find solidarity, guidance, and a sense of belonging.

Connecting with Like-Minded Organizations

One of the first steps in building alliances and networks is to connect with like-minded organizations and individuals who are also dedicated to exposing the truth behind Agenda 21 and Agenda 2030. These can include grassroots movements, advocacy groups, think tanks, and whistleblowers who have firsthand knowledge or evidence of the global genocide plan.

Online platforms and social media have made it easier than ever to find and connect with individuals and organizations that share similar goals. Utilize these platforms to reach out, share information, and collaborate on projects. By joining forces, we can amplify our message and reach a wider audience, increasing the chances of awakening more people to the truth.

Sharing Information and Resources

Another crucial aspect of building alliances and networks is the sharing of information and resources. In the age of information, knowledge is power, and by pooling our resources, we can gather a wealth of evidence, research studies, official documents, and testimonies that expose the truth behind Agenda 21 and Agenda 2030.

Establishing a centralized platform or website where individuals and organizations can contribute and access this information can be immensely valuable. This platform can serve as a hub for sharing research, reports, and insider accounts, making it easier for individuals to educate themselves and others about the global genocide plan. It can also provide a space for whistleblowers to come forward and share their experiences, ensuring that their voices are heard and their stories are documented.

Collaborative Projects and Actions

Building alliances and networks should not be limited to sharing information alone. Collaborative projects and actions can have a significant impact in raising awareness and challenging the global genocide agenda. These projects can include organizing conferences, seminars, and workshops to educate the public, lobbying policymakers, and engaging in legal challenges to protect individual liberties and constitutional rights.

By working together, we can also support and amplify the efforts of whistleblowers who have risked their careers and personal safety to expose the truth. Providing them with legal assistance, protection, and platforms to share their stories can help ensure that their voices are not silenced and that their revelations reach a wider audience.

Strengthening the Global Movement

Building alliances and networks is not limited to a single country or region. The global genocide agenda of Agenda 21 and Agenda 2030 affects people worldwide, and therefore, it is crucial to strengthen the global movement against it. Connecting with international organizations, activists, and researchers can provide a broader perspective and a more comprehensive understanding of the forces at play.

International collaborations can also help in pressuring governments and international bodies to address the concerns raised by the global genocide agenda. By presenting a united front, we can demand transparency, accountability, and the preservation of individual liberties and sovereignty.

Conclusion

Building alliances and networks is a vital component of the resistance against the global genocide agenda of Agenda 21 and Agenda 2030. By coming together, sharing information, and collaborating on projects and actions, we can amplify our voices, expose the truth, and work towards a better future for humanity. The power of unity and resistance cannot be underestimated, and it is through collective action that we can overcome the challenges posed by the deep state and their destructive plans.

8.4 Strategies for Overcoming Global Genocide

As we delve deeper into the sinister agenda of Agenda 21 and Agenda 2030, it becomes increasingly important to discuss strategies for overcoming the global genocide that is being planned and executed by the deep state and its collaborators. The fight against this evil plan requires a united front and a comprehensive approach. In this section, we will explore some strategies that can be employed to counteract and ultimately defeat this genocidal agenda.

1. Spreading Awareness

One of the most crucial strategies in combating global genocide is spreading awareness. The first step towards resistance is ensuring that people are informed about the true nature and intentions of Agenda 21 and Agenda 2030. This can be achieved through various means, such as writing articles, publishing books, creating documentaries, and utilizing social media platforms. By disseminating the truth, we can awaken the masses and empower them to take action against this heinous plan.

2. Educating Others

In addition to spreading awareness, it is essential to educate others about the documented facts and evidence surrounding Agenda 21 and Agenda 2030. By providing concrete evidence and presenting well-researched arguments, we can effectively counter the propaganda and misinformation that the deep state and its collaborators disseminate. Education is a powerful tool in dismantling the deception and manipulation employed by those behind this genocidal agenda.

3. Building Alliances and Networks

To effectively combat global genocide, it is crucial to build alliances and networks with like-minded individuals and organizations. By joining forces, we can amplify our voices and increase our impact. Collaborating with grassroots movements, human rights organizations, and other groups fighting against tyranny and oppression can strengthen our collective efforts. Together, we can create a formidable force that cannot be ignored or silenced.

4. Legal Challenges and Constitutional Rights

Utilizing legal challenges and asserting our constitutional rights is another important strategy in overcoming global genocide. By working with lawyers, activists, and organizations specializing in constitutional law, we can challenge the legality and legitimacy of the actions taken under the guise of Agenda 21 and Agenda 2030. This includes filing lawsuits, advocating for legislative changes, and demanding transparency and accountability from those in power.

5. Political Resistance and Grassroots Movements

Political resistance and grassroots movements play a vital role in countering the genocidal agenda. By actively participating in local, national, and international politics, we can elect representatives who are committed to preserving individual liberties and sovereignty. Grassroots movements can organize protests, rallies, and demonstrations to raise awareness and put pressure on governments to reject and abandon the destructive policies associated with Agenda 21 and Agenda 2030.

6. Whistleblowers and Leaks

Whistleblowers and leaks have historically played a significant role in exposing corruption and unveiling hidden agendas. Encouraging individuals within the deep state and other organizations involved in the implementation of Agenda 21 and Agenda 2030 to come forward with information can provide invaluable insights and evidence. Protecting and supporting whistleblowers is essential in uncovering the truth and holding those responsible accountable for their actions.

7. Preserving Individual Liberties and Sovereignty

Protecting and preserving individual liberties and sovereignty is paramount in the fight against global genocide. It is crucial to resist any attempts to erode our fundamental rights and freedoms under the guise of sustainable development or global governance. By advocating for limited government intervention, upholding the principles of individual liberty, and defending national sovereignty, we can safeguard ourselves against the encroachment of this genocidal agenda.

8. Peaceful Resistance and Civil Disobedience

Peaceful resistance and civil disobedience can be powerful tools in opposing the genocidal agenda. Engaging in nonviolent protests, boycotts, and acts of civil disobedience can disrupt the implementation of Agenda 21 and Agenda 2030. By refusing to comply with unjust laws and policies, we can send a strong message to those in power that we will not tolerate their attempts to control and manipulate us.

9. Creating Alternative Solutions and Visions

Offering alternative solutions and visions for a sustainable and free world is essential in countering the genocidal agenda. By promoting innovative ideas and practices that prioritize individual freedoms, environmental stewardship, and economic prosperity, we can present a compelling alternative to the destructive policies of Agenda 21 and Agenda 2030. By showcasing the viability and benefits of these alternatives, we can inspire others to reject the genocidal agenda and embrace a brighter future.

10. Hope for a Better Future

Finally, it is crucial to maintain hope for a better future. Despite the darkness and despair that surround the genocidal agenda, we must remember that humanity has overcome great challenges throughout history. By staying united, resilient, and committed to the cause, we can overcome the forces of evil and ensure a future that upholds the dignity, freedom, and well-being of all individuals.

In conclusion, the fight against global genocide requires a multifaceted approach. By spreading awareness, educating others, building alliances, utilizing legal challenges, engaging in political resistance, supporting whistleblowers, preserving individual liberties, practicing peaceful resistance, creating alternative solutions, and maintaining hope, we can overcome the genocidal agenda of Agenda 21 and Agenda 2030. Together, we can protect humanity and build a future that respects and values the inherent worth and rights of every individual.

The Fight for Freedom

9.1 Legal Challenges and Constitutional Rights

As the truth about Agenda 21 and Agenda 2030 continues to be exposed, concerned citizens around the world are seeking legal avenues to challenge and resist the implementation of these global plans. The fight for freedom and the preservation of constitutional rights has become a crucial aspect of the battle against the evil behind global genocide.

The Importance of Constitutional Rights

Constitutional rights form the foundation of a free and just society. They protect individuals from government overreach and ensure that the power remains in the hands of the people. In the face of Agenda 21 and Agenda 2030, it is essential to understand and assert these rights to safeguard our liberties.

One of the key challenges in combating the global genocide plan lies in the fact that it often operates under the guise of sustainable development and environmentalism. This allows proponents of these agendas to bypass constitutional protections and implement policies that infringe upon individual freedoms. However, by understanding our constitutional rights and utilizing legal strategies, we can push back against these encroachments.

Challenging the Legality of Agenda 21 and Agenda 2030

To effectively challenge the legality of Agenda 21 and Agenda 2030, it is crucial to examine the legal frameworks within which these plans operate. Many countries have constitutional provisions that protect individual rights, private property, and sovereignty. By analyzing these provisions, concerned citizens and legal experts can identify potential violations and develop legal arguments to challenge the implementation of these global agendas.

One avenue for legal challenges lies in the violation of property rights. Agenda 21 and Agenda 2030 often involve land grabbing and resource control, which can infringe upon the rights of individuals and communities. By highlighting these violations, legal challenges can be mounted to protect property rights and prevent the erosion of individual liberties.

Additionally, the push for global governance and the erosion of national sovereignty can be challenged on constitutional grounds. Many countries have constitutional provisions that protect the sovereignty of the nation and its citizens. By asserting these rights and highlighting the potential infringements caused by global governance, legal challenges can be mounted to protect the integrity of national governments and the rights of their citizens.

The Role of International Law

International law also plays a crucial role in challenging the legality of Agenda 21 and Agenda 2030. Treaties and agreements that promote sustainable development and environmental protection must be scrutinized to ensure they do not infringe upon individual rights or undermine national sovereignty.

Legal experts and concerned citizens can analyze these international agreements to identify potential conflicts with constitutional rights and national laws. By bringing attention to these conflicts, legal challenges can be mounted to prevent the implementation of policies that violate individual liberties and undermine national sovereignty.

Protecting Individual Liberties

In the fight against global genocide, it is essential to protect individual liberties and prevent the erosion of fundamental rights. This requires a vigilant and informed citizenry that is willing to stand up for their rights and challenge the implementation of oppressive policies.

One of the most effective ways to protect individual liberties is through grassroots movements and political resistance. By organizing and mobilizing, concerned citizens can bring attention to the dangers of Agenda 21 and Agenda 2030 and demand that their constitutional rights be upheld.

The Importance of Whistleblowers and Leaks

Whistleblowers play a crucial role in exposing the truth behind Agenda 21 and Agenda 2030. Their insider knowledge and willingness to come forward with evidence are invaluable in the fight against global genocide. Whistleblowers provide the necessary proof to back up claims and expose the individuals and organizations involved in drafting, endorsing, and promoting these agendas.

Leaks of official documents and insider accounts also contribute to the understanding of the true intentions behind Agenda 21 and Agenda 2030. These leaks provide concrete evidence that can be used in legal challenges and further expose the evil behind global genocide.

Conclusion

Legal challenges and the assertion of constitutional rights are essential in the fight against Agenda 21 and Agenda 2030. By understanding and utilizing the legal frameworks within which these global plans operate, concerned citizens can mount effective challenges to protect individual liberties, property rights, and national sovereignty. The role of whistleblowers and leaks cannot be overstated, as they provide the evidence necessary to expose the truth and hold those responsible accountable. It is through these legal challenges and the preservation of constitutional rights that we can hope to overcome the evil behind global genocide and create a sustainable and free world for future generations.

9.2 Political Resistance and Grassroots Movements

Political resistance and grassroots movements play a crucial role in challenging and countering the insidious agenda of global genocide outlined in Agenda 21 and Agenda 2030. As more individuals become aware of the true intentions behind these plans, they are joining forces to expose the truth, protect their freedoms, and fight for a better future.

The Power of Political Resistance

Political resistance is a powerful tool in the fight against global genocide. It involves individuals and groups actively opposing the implementation of Agenda 21 and Agenda 2030 through various means, including peaceful protests, lobbying, and legal challenges. By raising awareness and mobilizing others, political resistance aims to disrupt the plans of the global elite and protect the rights and liberties of individuals and communities.

One of the key aspects of political resistance is the ability to expose the true nature of Agenda 21 and Agenda 2030. Whistleblowers, like the one who provided the information for this book, play a crucial role in revealing the hidden agenda and providing evidence to support their claims. Their courage and willingness to speak out against powerful forces are essential in awakening the masses and inspiring political resistance.

Grassroots Movements: Uniting for Change

Grassroots movements are another vital component of the resistance against global genocide. These movements are characterized by their bottom-up approach, where individuals and communities come together to address common concerns and advocate for change. Grassroots movements are often driven by passionate individuals who are deeply committed to preserving their freedoms and protecting their communities.

These movements can take various forms, from local community organizations to national and international networks. They provide a platform for individuals to share information, organize events, and collaborate on strategies to counter the agenda of global genocide. Grassroots movements empower individuals to take action and make a difference in their own communities.

Strategies for Political Resistance

Political resistance and grassroots movements employ a range of strategies to challenge the implementation of Agenda 21 and Agenda 2030. Some of these strategies include:

1. **Education and Awareness**: Spreading knowledge and raising awareness about the true intentions behind Agenda 21 and Agenda 2030 is crucial. By educating others about the dangers of these plans, individuals can inspire others to join the resistance and take action.
2. **Building Alliances**: Collaboration and building alliances with like-minded individuals and organizations are essential for a strong resistance movement. By working together, individuals can pool their resources, share information, and amplify their voices.
3. **Legal Challenges**: Challenging the legality of policies and regulations associated with Agenda 21 and Agenda 2030 can be an effective strategy. By utilizing legal avenues, individuals and organizations can hold governments and institutions accountable for their actions and potentially halt the implementation of harmful policies.
4. **Political Engagement**: Engaging with political processes and institutions is another way to resist the agenda of global genocide. This can involve running for office, supporting candidates who align with the values of freedom and sovereignty, and actively participating in local and national politics.
5. **Peaceful Protests**: Peaceful protests and demonstrations can draw attention to the issues at hand and put pressure on governments and institutions to reconsider their support for Agenda 21 and Agenda

2030. These protests can range from small local gatherings to large-scale national or international events.

The Role of Whistleblowers and Leaks

Whistleblowers play a critical role in exposing the truth behind Agenda 21 and Agenda 2030. Their insider knowledge and evidence provide valuable insights into the hidden agenda and the methods employed to achieve global genocide. Whistleblowers often risk their careers, reputations, and even their personal safety to bring this information to light.

Leaks of official documents and insider accounts provide concrete evidence that supports the claims made by whistleblowers. These leaks serve as a wake-up call to the public, revealing the true intentions and strategies of the global elite. They empower individuals and organizations to take action, demand transparency, and resist the implementation of harmful policies.

Preserving Individual Liberties and Sovereignty

At the heart of political resistance and grassroots movements is the preservation of individual liberties and national sovereignty. The fight against global genocide is ultimately a fight for freedom, autonomy, and the right to determine one's own destiny. By resisting the implementation of Agenda 21 and Agenda 2030, individuals and communities are asserting their right to self-governance and rejecting the imposition of a globalist agenda.

Political resistance and grassroots movements are essential in safeguarding the principles of democracy, individual rights, and national sovereignty. They provide hope for a future where individuals can live free from the oppressive control of the global elite. Through unity, awareness, and action, individuals can work together to create a sustainable and free world for future generations.

In the next section, we will explore the role of legal challenges and constitutional rights in the fight against global genocide.

9.3 The Role of Whistleblowers and Leaks

Whistleblowers play a crucial role in exposing the truth behind hidden agendas and shedding light on the dark intentions of those in power. In the case of Agenda 21 and Agenda 2030, whistleblowers have been instrumental in uncovering the sinister plans for global genocide. These brave individuals have risked their careers, reputations, and even their lives to bring forth the evidence and proof that the world needs to see.

Whistleblowers have provided invaluable insights into the drafting process of Agenda 21 and Agenda 2030. They have revealed the names of those responsible for crafting these plans, exposing the individuals who have meticulously designed a blueprint for global control and population reduction. By shining a light on the drafters, whistleblowers have allowed us to understand the motivations and ideologies behind these agendas.

Furthermore, whistleblowers have exposed the endorsers and promoters of Agenda 21 and Agenda 2030. These individuals, often influential figures in politics, business, and academia, have actively supported and advocated for the implementation of these plans. By revealing their names, whistleblowers have exposed the web of power and influence that perpetuates the global genocide agenda.

The information provided by whistleblowers goes beyond mere accusations; it is backed by documented facts and evidence. These brave individuals have risked their personal safety to leak official documents, research studies, and insider accounts that corroborate the existence and intentions of Agenda 21 and Agenda 2030. Through their leaks, whistleblowers have provided the public with tangible proof, allowing us to see the truth for ourselves.

The role of whistleblowers in exposing the deep state's agenda cannot be overstated. They have revealed the methods of population control that the global elite plan to employ. From economic warfare and financial manipulation to the exploitation of environmental concerns, whistleblowers have exposed the intricate web of strategies designed to subjugate and control the masses. Their leaks have allowed us to understand the true extent of the global genocide plan.

Whistleblowers have also played a crucial role in exposing the deception and manipulation tactics employed by those pushing the agenda. They have revealed the propaganda and misinformation campaigns that seek to shape public opinion and silence dissenting voices. By exposing the media's role in perpetuating the agenda, whistleblowers have highlighted the importance of critical thinking and independent research in the face of a controlled narrative.

In addition to exposing the agenda, whistleblowers have shed light on the mechanisms of resistance and awakening. They have emphasized the power of awareness and the urgency of spreading the truth. By sharing their knowledge and experiences, whistleblowers have inspired others to take a stand against global genocide. They have encouraged the formation of alliances and networks, fostering a sense of unity and collective action.

Whistleblowers have also played a crucial role in legal challenges and the preservation of constitutional rights. By providing evidence and testimonies, they have supported legal efforts to expose and challenge the agenda. Their leaks have empowered individuals and grassroots movements to resist the encroachment on their individual liberties and sovereignty.

It is important to recognize and protect the role of whistleblowers in our society. Their courage and sacrifice should be acknowledged and celebrated. Whistleblowers are the unsung heroes who risk everything to expose the truth and fight for a better future. Their leaks have provided us with the knowledge and evidence needed to resist the global genocide agenda and work towards creating a sustainable and free world.

In conclusion, whistleblowers have played a pivotal role in unveiling the evil behind global genocide as outlined in Agenda 21 and Agenda 2030. Their leaks have exposed the drafters, endorsers, and promoters of these agendas, providing documented facts and evidence to support their claims. Whistleblowers have shed light on the methods of population control, the deception and manipulation tactics employed, and the mechanisms of resistance and awakening. Their bravery and sacrifice should be recognized as they continue to play a vital role in preserving individual liberties and sovereignty in the fight against global genocide.

9.4 Preserving Individual Liberties and Sovereignty

As we delve deeper into the sinister agenda of Agenda 21 and Agenda 2030, it becomes increasingly crucial to discuss the preservation of individual liberties and sovereignty. In the face of global genocide, it is imperative that we stand united to protect our fundamental rights and freedoms. This section will explore the strategies and actions we can take to safeguard our individual liberties and maintain our sovereignty in the face of this grave threat.

The Importance of Individual Liberties

Individual liberties are the cornerstone of any free society. They encompass our rights to freedom of speech, assembly, religion, and the pursuit of happiness. These liberties are not granted by any government or international organization; they are inherent to every human being. However, the proponents of Agenda 21 and Agenda 2030 seek to undermine these fundamental rights in their pursuit of global control.

Preserving individual liberties requires a vigilant and informed citizenry. We must educate ourselves about the true intentions behind these agendas and the tactics employed to erode our freedoms. By staying informed and engaged, we can resist the encroachment on our liberties and protect the values that define us as free individuals.

Upholding Sovereignty

Sovereignty is the essence of self-governance and the ability of a nation to make decisions in its own best interest. The globalists behind Agenda 21 and Agenda 2030 aim to dismantle national sovereignty and replace it with a system of global governance. This would strip nations of their autonomy and subject them to the whims of unelected bureaucrats.

To preserve our sovereignty, we must reject the notion of global governance and assert our rights as independent nations. This requires a strong commitment to national identity and a refusal to surrender our decision-making power to supranational entities. We must resist any attempts to undermine our sovereignty and assert our right to determine our own destiny.

Strengthening Legal Protections

One of the most effective ways to preserve individual liberties and sovereignty is through the strengthening of legal protections. We must ensure that our legal systems are robust enough to withstand the encroachments of globalist agendas. This includes safeguarding our constitutional rights, promoting transparency and accountability, and holding those in power accountable for their actions.

Citizens must actively engage in the political process, supporting candidates who prioritize individual liberties and sovereignty. We must demand that our elected officials uphold their oaths to protect and defend the constitution. By participating in grassroots movements and advocating for legal reforms, we can create a legal framework that safeguards our freedoms and prevents the erosion of our sovereignty.

Promoting Economic Independence

Economic independence is closely tied to individual liberties and sovereignty. The globalists behind Agenda 21 and Agenda 2030 seek to create a system of financial manipulation and dependency that would render nations and individuals subservient to their agenda. To counter this, we must promote economic independence and self-sufficiency.

Supporting local businesses, investing in domestic industries, and reducing reliance on multinational corporations are all steps towards economic independence. By fostering a strong and resilient economy, we can protect our sovereignty and ensure that our decisions are not dictated by external forces. Additionally, promoting fair trade practices and resisting exploitative economic policies will help preserve our individual liberties and prevent the concentration of wealth in the hands of a few.

Building Alliances and Networks

Preserving individual liberties and sovereignty requires collective action. We must build alliances and networks with like-minded individuals and organizations to amplify our voices and increase our impact. By joining forces, we can pool our resources, share information, and coordinate efforts to counter the globalist agenda.

Networking with whistleblowers, activists, and researchers who have exposed the truth behind Agenda 21 and Agenda 2030 is crucial. Their insights and evidence can help us strengthen our arguments and expose the true nature of these agendas to a wider audience. By collaborating with others who share our concerns, we can create a united front against global genocide and work towards a future that respects individual liberties and national sovereignty.

Conclusion

Preserving individual liberties and sovereignty is paramount in the face of the global genocide plan outlined in Agenda 21 and Agenda 2030. By staying informed, upholding our rights, and actively participating in the political process, we can protect our freedoms and resist the encroachment of globalist agendas. It is through collective action and a steadfast commitment to our values that we can ensure a future that respects the dignity and sovereignty of every individual.

The Future of Humanity

10.1 The Consequences of Inaction

As we delve deeper into the sinister agenda of Agenda 21 and Agenda 2030, it becomes increasingly crucial to understand the dire consequences of inaction. The global genocide plan orchestrated by the deep state and its collaborators is not a mere conspiracy theory; it is a chilling reality that threatens the very existence of humanity. In this section, we will explore the potential ramifications of turning a blind eye to this nefarious agenda.

The first and most obvious consequence of inaction is the loss of countless innocent lives. The architects of Agenda 21 and Agenda 2030 have devised methods of population control that are both insidious and effective. Through various means such as forced sterilizations, mass vaccinations, and the manipulation of healthcare access, they aim to reduce the global population to a manageable level. If we fail to expose and resist these tactics, we risk allowing the deep state to carry out their genocidal plans unhindered.

Furthermore, the consequences of inaction extend beyond the immediate loss of life. The destruction of national economies, as outlined in Chapter 4, will lead to widespread poverty, unemployment, and social unrest. The rise of global governance, facilitated by financial manipulation and dependency, will strip nations of their sovereignty and render citizens powerless against the oppressive forces at play. By remaining passive, we surrender our freedom and allow the elite to consolidate their power and wealth at the expense of the masses.

Inaction also perpetuates the deception and manipulation that underpin Agenda 21 and Agenda 2030. The propagandistic machinery employed by the deep state relies on the apathy and ignorance of the masses. By failing to challenge the false narratives of climate change, green energy scams, and environmental concerns, we become complicit in the perpetuation of these lies. The media's role in disseminating misinformation and silencing truth seekers is further reinforced when we choose not to resist. Inaction allows the brainwashing of the masses to continue unchecked, creating a generation of compliant citizens who are unaware of the true agenda at hand.

Moreover, the consequences of inaction extend to the realm of education and indoctrination. By failing to resist the reprogramming of our youth through initiatives like Common Core and globalist curriculum, we condemn future generations to a life devoid of critical thinking and independent thought. Inaction allows the suppression of dissenting voices and the creation of a compliant populace that is easily manipulated and controlled. By not taking a stand against the indoctrination of our children, we contribute to the erosion of individual liberties and the perpetuation of the deep state's agenda.

Inaction also has severe implications for healthcare and population control. The pharmaceutical industry, complicit in the deep state's plans, plays a pivotal role in depopulation efforts through the promotion of vaccines and the suppression of alternative treatments. By remaining passive, we allow the erosion of reproductive rights and the implementation of eugenics programs that seek to control and manipulate human reproduction. Inaction also enables the deep state to control healthcare access and quality, ensuring that only those deemed worthy by their standards receive adequate care. By failing to resist these measures, we jeopardize the health and well-being of future generations.

The consequences of inaction are dire, but they are not insurmountable. It is essential to recognize that we have the power to resist and overcome the global genocide plan outlined in Agenda 21 and Agenda 2030. By raising awareness, exposing the agenda, and building alliances and networks, we can create a formidable force against the deep state's machinations. The fight for freedom requires legal challenges, political resistance, and grassroots movements. Whistleblowers and leaks play a crucial role in uncovering the truth and preserving individual liberties and sovereignty.

In conclusion, the consequences of inaction are far-reaching and devastating. By turning a blind eye to the global genocide plan outlined in Agenda 21 and Agenda 2030, we risk the loss of countless lives, the destruction of national economies, the erosion of individual liberties, and the perpetuation of a manipulative and oppressive system. However, there is hope. By taking a stand, spreading awareness, and uniting against this nefarious agenda, we can create a sustainable and free world for future generations. The power lies in our hands, and it is up to us to determine the course of humanity's future.

10.2 Creating a Sustainable and Free World

As we have delved deep into the dark underbelly of Agenda 21 and Agenda 2030, exposing the evil intentions behind global genocide, it is crucial to shift our focus towards creating a sustainable and free world. While the revelations we have uncovered may leave us feeling disheartened and overwhelmed, it is essential to remember that knowledge is power. Armed with the truth, we can work towards dismantling this nefarious agenda and building a better future for humanity.

The Power of Awareness

One of the most critical steps in creating a sustainable and free world is spreading awareness. We must continue to educate ourselves and others about the true nature of Agenda 21 and Agenda 2030. By sharing the knowledge we have gained, we can awaken others to the dangers that lie ahead. Awareness is the first step towards mobilizing individuals and communities to take action against this global genocide plan.

Grassroots Movements and Political Resistance

Creating a sustainable and free world requires collective action. Grassroots movements play a vital role in challenging the status quo and advocating for change. By organizing at the local level, we can build a strong foundation for resistance against the implementation of Agenda 21 and Agenda 2030. Grassroots movements have the power to influence political discourse, hold elected officials accountable, and shape policies that prioritize individual liberties and sovereignty.

Political resistance is another crucial aspect of creating a sustainable and free world. We must actively engage in the political process, supporting candidates who are committed to preserving our constitutional rights and rejecting the globalist agenda. By participating in elections, voicing our concerns, and demanding transparency, we can ensure that our voices are heard and our interests are represented.

The Role of Whistleblowers and Leaks

Throughout history, whistleblowers have played a pivotal role in exposing corruption and unveiling hidden agendas. Whistleblowers possess insider knowledge and firsthand accounts that can provide irrefutable evidence of the true intentions behind Agenda 21 and Agenda 2030. Their courage to come forward and reveal the truth is instrumental in our fight against global genocide.

We must support and protect whistleblowers, creating an environment where they feel safe to share their experiences and evidence. By amplifying their voices and demanding accountability, we can shed light on the dark secrets of those who drafted and endorse these genocidal plans. Whistleblowers are the catalysts for change, and their contributions are invaluable in our quest for a sustainable and free world.

Preserving Individual Liberties and Sovereignty

At the heart of creating a sustainable and free world lies the preservation of individual liberties and sovereignty. We must fiercely protect our rights to life, liberty, and the pursuit of happiness. This includes safeguarding our freedom of speech, assembly, and privacy. It also means resisting any attempts to erode our national sovereignty and subject us to global governance.

To achieve this, we must actively engage in the political process, supporting candidates who prioritize individual liberties and sovereignty. We must also advocate for the preservation of our constitutional rights through legal challenges and grassroots movements. By standing united and unwavering in our commitment to freedom, we can ensure that future generations inherit a world that values and protects their individual rights.

Hope for a Better Future

While the revelations surrounding Agenda 21 and Agenda 2030 may seem bleak, we must not lose hope. The power of the human spirit and our collective determination to create a better world can overcome any obstacle. By working together, spreading awareness, and actively resisting the global genocide plan, we can pave the way for a future that is sustainable, free, and filled with hope.

In conclusion, creating a sustainable and free world requires our unwavering commitment to spreading awareness, engaging in grassroots movements, supporting political resistance, protecting whistleblowers, and preserving individual liberties and sovereignty. It is through these collective efforts that we can dismantle the evil behind Agenda 21 and Agenda 2030 and build a future where humanity thrives. The time for action is now, and together, we can overcome the forces of global genocide and create a world that cherishes life, freedom, and justice for all.

10.3 Alternative Solutions and Visions

While it is crucial to expose the truth behind Agenda 21 and Agenda 2030, it is equally important to explore alternative solutions and visions for a sustainable and free world. In this section, we will discuss some ideas and strategies that can help counteract the global genocide plan and create a better future for humanity.

1. Promoting Individual Liberties and Sovereignty

One of the key aspects of resisting the global genocide plan is to uphold and protect individual liberties and sovereignty. It is essential to recognize the importance of personal freedom and the right to make choices that align with one's values and beliefs. By advocating for individual liberties, we can create a society that respects and values the autonomy of its citizens.

2. Strengthening Local Communities

Building strong and resilient local communities is another crucial step towards countering the global genocide plan. By fostering a sense of community and promoting self-sufficiency, we can reduce our dependence on centralized systems and institutions. Encouraging local food production, community-based healthcare initiatives, and sustainable energy solutions can empower communities and create a more resilient society.

3. Embracing Sustainable Practices

Transitioning towards sustainable practices is essential for creating a better future. This includes adopting renewable energy sources, promoting eco-friendly transportation, and implementing sustainable agricultural methods. By reducing our carbon footprint and preserving natural resources, we can mitigate the environmental impact and create a more sustainable world for future generations.

4. Educating and Empowering the Youth

Investing in the education and empowerment of the youth is crucial for countering the global genocide plan. By providing them with critical thinking skills, promoting independent thought, and encouraging them to question authority, we can create a generation of informed and engaged individuals. It is essential to teach them about the true nature of Agenda 21 and Agenda 2030, empowering them to make informed decisions and actively participate in shaping their future.

5. Supporting Whistleblowers and Leaks

Whistleblowers play a vital role in exposing the truth and holding those responsible accountable. It is crucial to support and protect whistleblowers who come forward with valuable information about the global genocide plan. By creating safe spaces for whistleblowers to share their knowledge and experiences, we can ensure that the truth continues to be revealed, and the perpetrators are brought to justice.

6. Strengthening International Alliances

Creating strong international alliances is essential for countering the global genocide plan. By collaborating with like-minded individuals, organizations, and governments across the world, we can amplify our efforts and create a united front against the forces behind Agenda 21 and Agenda 2030. Sharing information, resources, and strategies can help us build a global movement that stands against global genocide and works towards a sustainable and free world.

7. Promoting Transparency and Accountability

Transparency and accountability are crucial in countering the global genocide plan. It is essential to demand transparency from governments, institutions, and organizations involved in implementing Agenda 21 and Agenda 2030. Holding them accountable for their actions and ensuring that they operate in the best interests of the people is vital for safeguarding our future.

8. Raising Awareness and Spreading Information

Continuing to raise awareness and spread information about the true nature of Agenda 21 and Agenda 2030 is essential. By utilizing various platforms such as social media, grassroots movements, and alternative media outlets, we can reach a wider audience and educate them about the global genocide plan. It is crucial to provide evidence-based information and encourage critical thinking to counter the propaganda and misinformation surrounding these agendas.

9. Engaging in Political Resistance

Political resistance is a powerful tool in countering the global genocide plan. By actively participating in the political process, supporting candidates who prioritize individual liberties and sovereignty, and advocating for policies that align with our values, we can create meaningful change. It is essential to engage in peaceful protests, petitions, and grassroots movements to voice our concerns and demand accountability from our elected officials.

10. Cultivating Hope and Unity

Lastly, cultivating hope and unity is crucial in the fight against global genocide. It is essential to remember that we are not alone in this struggle and that there are countless individuals around the world who share our concerns. By coming together, supporting one another, and fostering a sense of unity, we can create a powerful force that can challenge the global genocide plan and work towards a better future for humanity.

In conclusion, while exposing the truth behind Agenda 21 and Agenda 2030 is essential, it is equally important to explore alternative solutions and visions for a sustainable and free world. By promoting individual liberties, strengthening local communities, embracing sustainable practices, educating and empowering the youth, supporting whistleblowers, strengthening international alliances, promoting transparency and accountability, raising awareness, engaging in political resistance, and cultivating hope and unity, we can counter the global genocide plan and create a better future for humanity.

10.4 Hope for a Better Future

In the face of the dark and sinister agenda laid out by Agenda 21 and Agenda 2030, it is easy to feel overwhelmed and hopeless. The global genocide plan, orchestrated by the deep state and its collaborators, seems insurmountable. However, even in the midst of this darkness, there is still hope for a better future.

The first glimmer of hope lies in the power of awareness. As more and more individuals become informed about the true intentions behind Agenda 21 and Agenda 2030, the potential for resistance and change grows exponentially. It is through awareness that we can expose the lies and propaganda that have been used to manipulate the masses. By sharing the truth with others, we can awaken a collective consciousness that is ready to fight for freedom and justice.

But awareness alone is not enough. It is crucial that we take action and expose the agenda to as many people as possible. We must be courageous whistleblowers, unafraid to speak out against the atrocities being planned and executed by those in power. By providing concrete evidence and documented facts, we can dismantle the web of deception that has been woven around us.

Building alliances and networks is another key aspect of our fight against global genocide. We must come together, regardless of our differences, to form a united front against the forces that seek to destroy humanity. By collaborating with like-minded individuals and organizations, we can amplify our voices and increase our impact. Together, we can create a powerful movement that cannot be ignored.

In our struggle for a better future, it is essential to develop strategies that will help us overcome the challenges we face. We must be resilient and adaptable, constantly evolving our tactics to stay one step ahead of the oppressors. By studying their methods and understanding their weaknesses, we can devise effective countermeasures that will undermine their plans for global domination.

One of the most important strategies for overcoming global genocide is preserving individual liberties and sovereignty. We must fiercely protect our rights and freedoms, refusing to succumb to the control and manipulation of the deep state. By asserting our autonomy and asserting our right to self-determination, we can create a world where every individual is free to live according to their own values and beliefs.

Education and enlightenment play a crucial role in shaping a better future. We must reprogram the youth, teaching them critical thinking skills and empowering them to question authority. By exposing the flaws in the globalist curriculum, such as Common Core, we can ensure that future generations are not indoctrinated into a system that seeks to suppress their individuality and creativity.

Furthermore, we must strive to create a generation of citizens who are not only aware of the agenda but also actively engaged in resisting it. By fostering a sense of responsibility and empowerment, we can inspire individuals to take a stand against global genocide. Through grassroots movements and political resistance, we can reclaim our power and shape a future that is free from the shackles of oppression.

While the fight against global genocide may seem daunting, we must remember that history is filled with examples of triumph over tyranny. Throughout the ages, individuals and communities have risen up against oppressive regimes and fought for their freedom. We must draw inspiration from these stories and believe in our ability to create a better world.

In conclusion, despite the darkness that surrounds us, there is still hope for a better future. Through awareness, action, and unity, we can expose the true intentions behind Agenda 21 and Agenda 2030. By preserving our individual liberties and sovereignty, we can resist the forces that seek to control and manipulate us. Through education and enlightenment, we can empower future generations to question authority and fight for their freedom. Together, we have the power to overcome global genocide and create a sustainable and free world for all.

Conclusion

11.1 Recapitulating the Exposed Truth

Throughout this book, we have delved deep into the dark underbelly of Agenda 21 and Agenda 2030, uncovering the sinister plans and hidden agendas behind these global initiatives. We have heard the whistleblower's perspective, exposing the truth from someone who has seen the inner workings of this malevolent plan. We have unmasked the drafters of Agenda 21, shedding light on the individuals responsible for crafting this blueprint for global genocide. And we have revealed the names of those who endorse and promote this insidious agenda, exposing their true intentions.

The deep state's agenda, as we have discovered, is to exert control over the world's population through various methods of population control. From the manipulation of economic systems to the suppression of critical thinking, they have devised a multi-faceted approach to achieve their desired outcome. The numbers game they play is one of manipulation and deception, using statistics and data to justify their actions while hiding their true intentions.

But we have not relied solely on speculation and conjecture. No, we have presented documented facts and evidence to support our claims. We have examined official documents and agendas, research studies and reports, and testimonies from insiders who have bravely come forward to expose the truth. The evidence is overwhelming, and it cannot be ignored.

Propaganda and misinformation have played a significant role in advancing the agenda of global genocide. The media, as we have seen, has been complicit in spreading the false narrative of climate change and promoting the green energy scams associated with Agenda 21. They have been instrumental in brainwashing the masses, shaping public opinion, and silencing those who dare to question the official narrative.

Economic warfare and control have been key strategies employed by the elite to further their agenda. The destruction of national economies, the rise of global governance, financial manipulation, and wealth redistribution are all part of their grand plan. By creating dependency and exploiting economic vulnerabilities, they seek to consolidate power and control over the world's resources.

Environmentalism has been used as a tool to manipulate public sentiment and justify their actions. The false narrative of climate change has been perpetuated to instill fear and guilt in the population, paving the way for the implementation of Agenda 21. Green energy scams and land grabbing have been employed to gain control over valuable resources, while exploiting genuine environmental concerns for their own gain.

Education and indoctrination have been crucial in shaping the minds of future generations. Reprogramming the youth through initiatives like Common Core and globalist curriculum has been a deliberate strategy to suppress critical thinking and create a generation of compliant citizens. By controlling the education system, they ensure that their agenda is perpetuated and resistance is quashed.

Healthcare and population control have also been part of their grand scheme. The pharmaceutical industry, with its profit-driven motives, has played a significant role in advancing their agenda. Vaccines have been used as a means of depopulation, while reproductive rights and eugenics have been employed to control population growth. Access to healthcare and its quality have been manipulated to further their goals.

But amidst all the darkness, there is hope. We have explored the power of awareness and the importance of exposing the agenda. By building alliances and networks, we can stand united against global genocide. Strategies for overcoming this evil have been discussed, emphasizing the need for resistance and awakening.

Legal challenges and the preservation of constitutional rights are essential in the fight for freedom. Political resistance and grassroots movements have the potential to bring about real change. Whistleblowers and leaks have played a crucial role in exposing the truth, and their contributions should be acknowledged and protected. Preserving individual liberties and sovereignty is paramount in securing a better future for humanity.

In conclusion, the truth behind Agenda 21 and Agenda 2030 has been laid bare. We have recapitulated the exposed truth, highlighting the deep state's agenda, the methods of population control, the documented facts and evidence, and the role of propaganda and manipulation. We have emphasized the urgency of spreading awareness and the need to take a stand against global genocide. And we have recognized the power of unity and resistance in the fight for a sustainable and free world. The time for action is now.

11.2 The Urgency of Spreading Awareness

As we delve deeper into the sinister agenda of Agenda 21 and Agenda 2030, it becomes increasingly clear that time is of the essence. The urgency to spread awareness about the true nature of these global initiatives cannot be overstated. The future of humanity hangs in the balance, and it is our responsibility to expose the evil behind the veil of deception.

The whistleblowers who have come forward with their warnings have risked everything to bring the truth to light. They have provided us with invaluable proof and evidence that cannot be ignored. Their courage in speaking out against the powerful forces behind Agenda 21 and Agenda 2030 is commendable, and it is our duty to amplify their voices.

One of the most crucial aspects of spreading awareness is calling out the individuals who drafted these agendas. By revealing their names and exposing their intentions, we can shine a light on the architects of global genocide. These individuals must be held accountable for their actions and the devastating consequences they seek to unleash upon the world.

Equally important is unmasking the endorsers and promoters of Agenda 21 and Agenda 2030. These are the influential figures who lend their support to these destructive plans, either out of ignorance or a sinister agenda of their own. By exposing their involvement, we can challenge their credibility and disrupt the web of deceit that they have woven.

The deep state's agenda, intricately intertwined with Agenda 21 and Agenda 2030, must be brought to the forefront of public consciousness. This shadowy network of powerful individuals and institutions seeks to control and manipulate the global population for their own nefarious purposes. Their methods of population control are insidious and far-reaching, and they must be exposed for what they truly are.

The numbers game that the deep state plays is a chilling aspect of their plan. They aim to achieve a significant reduction in the global population, using various means to accomplish this goal. Whether it be through forced sterilization, mass vaccinations, or engineered economic crises, their tactics are designed to systematically eliminate vast numbers of people. The scale of their ambition is staggering, and it is imperative that we confront this reality head-on.

Documented facts and evidence are the backbone of our fight against the global genocide plan. We must compile and disseminate irrefutable proof of the atrocities being committed in the name of Agenda 21 and Agenda 2030. From leaked documents to testimonies from insiders, every piece of evidence serves to strengthen our case and expose the truth to those who have been deceived.

The urgency of spreading awareness cannot be overstated. Time is running out, and the consequences of inaction are dire. We must reach as many people as possible, awakening them to the imminent threat that Agenda 21 and Agenda 2030 pose to our freedom, sovereignty, and very existence.

Through various channels, such as social media, grassroots movements, and alternative media outlets, we can bypass the mainstream narrative and reach those who are still unaware of the true nature of these agendas. We must break through the walls of propaganda and misinformation that have been erected to shield the public from the harsh reality.

By building alliances and networks with like-minded individuals and organizations, we can amplify our message and create a united front against global genocide. Together, we can pool our resources, knowledge, and expertise to counter the deep state's agenda and protect the future of humanity.

Strategies for overcoming global genocide must be developed and implemented. We must educate ourselves and others about our constitutional rights, legal challenges, and political resistance. Grassroots movements can exert pressure on governments and institutions, demanding transparency and accountability. Whistleblowers and leaks play a crucial role in exposing the truth and must be protected and supported.

In conclusion, the urgency of spreading awareness about Agenda 21 and Agenda 2030 cannot be overstated. We must expose the architects, endorsers, and promoters of these agendas, as well as the deep state's sinister plans for global genocide. Armed with documented facts and evidence, we must awaken the masses, build alliances, and develop strategies for resistance. The future of humanity depends on our collective action and unwavering determination to preserve our freedom, sovereignty, and right to a better future.

11.3 Taking a Stand Against Global Genocide

As we delve deeper into the sinister agenda of Agenda 21 and Agenda 2030, it becomes increasingly crucial for us to take a stand against the global genocide that is being planned and executed by the powerful elites. The time for complacency and ignorance is over. We must rise up, unite, and fight for the preservation of humanity and our individual liberties.

The Whistleblower's Warning

The truth about Agenda 21 and Agenda 2030 has been brought to light by brave whistleblowers who have risked their lives and livelihoods to expose the dark secrets hidden within these global initiatives. These courageous individuals have provided us with invaluable insights and evidence, shedding light on the true intentions of the architects of this genocidal plan.

Through their testimonies and insider accounts, we have gained a deeper understanding of the methods and strategies employed by the deep state to carry out their agenda. They have revealed the names of those who drafted these plans, exposing their true intentions and the devastating consequences they seek to impose upon the world.

Exposing the Drafters

The drafters of Agenda 21 and Agenda 2030 are not faceless entities. They are real individuals with names and positions of power. By exposing these individuals, we can hold them accountable for their actions and ensure that their plans for global genocide do not go unnoticed or unchallenged.

Through meticulous research and investigation, we have uncovered the identities of these architects of destruction. Their names are now etched in the annals of history, forever associated with the heinous crimes they have committed against humanity. It is our duty to expose them to the world, to shine a light on their dark deeds, and to prevent them from furthering their genocidal agenda.

Unmasking the Endorsers and Promoters

The drafters of Agenda 21 and Agenda 2030 are not alone in their quest for global genocide. They have garnered support from various individuals and organizations who endorse and promote their nefarious plans. These endorsers and promoters play a crucial role in spreading the propaganda and misinformation necessary to manipulate the masses and silence dissenting voices.

By unmasking these endorsers and promoters, we can expose their complicity in this grand scheme of global genocide. We can challenge their narratives and reveal the true intentions behind their seemingly benevolent actions. It is through this exposure that we can awaken the masses to the dangers that lie ahead and rally them to join us in the fight against this evil agenda.

The Urgency of Taking a Stand

The urgency of taking a stand against global genocide cannot be overstated. The architects of Agenda 21 and Agenda 2030 have set ambitious targets for population control, seeking to reduce the world's population to a fraction of its current size. The numbers they hope to achieve are staggering, and the consequences for humanity are unimaginable.

We must act now to prevent this catastrophic future from becoming a reality. We cannot afford to be passive observers or victims of this genocidal plan. We must resist, expose, and challenge the architects and endorsers of this agenda at every turn. Our collective voice and actions have the power to disrupt their plans and protect the future of humanity.

The Power of Unity and Resistance

In the face of such overwhelming darkness, it is easy to feel powerless and insignificant. However, we must remember that we are not alone in this fight. There are millions of individuals around the world who share our concerns and are willing to stand up against global genocide.

By building alliances and networks, we can amplify our voices and increase our impact. Together, we can create a united front against the architects of Agenda 21 and Agenda 2030. Through peaceful resistance, civil disobedience, and the dissemination of truth, we can dismantle their plans and pave the way for a brighter future.

Conclusion

Taking a stand against global genocide is not a choice; it is a moral imperative. We must heed the warnings of whistleblowers, expose the drafters, endorsers, and promoters of Agenda 21 and Agenda 2030, and unite in our fight for the preservation of humanity. The time for action is now. Together, we can overcome this evil agenda and create a world where freedom, liberty, and the sanctity of life are cherished and protected.

11.4 The Power of Unity and Resistance

In the face of the daunting agenda laid out by Agenda 21 and Agenda 2030, it is crucial for individuals to recognize the power of unity and resistance. The global genocide plan orchestrated by the deep state and its collaborators can only be thwarted through a collective effort to expose the truth and stand against it. This section explores the importance of unity and resistance in the fight against global genocide.

The Strength in Unity

Unity is a force that can bring about significant change. When individuals come together, their collective voices become louder and more impactful. It is through unity that we can challenge the narratives and agendas pushed by those in power. By standing together, we can create a powerful movement that demands transparency, accountability, and justice.

The first step towards unity is awareness. It is essential for individuals to educate themselves about the true intentions behind Agenda 21 and Agenda 2030. By understanding the depth of the global genocide plan, people can unite under a common cause and work towards exposing the truth. This awareness can be spread through various means, such as social media, grassroots movements, and community gatherings.

Resistance: Exposing the Truth

Resistance is a vital component of the fight against global genocide. It involves actively challenging the narratives and propaganda perpetuated by the deep state and its collaborators. Resistance can take many forms, including peaceful protests, civil disobedience, and legal challenges. By refusing to accept the status quo, individuals can disrupt the plans of those seeking to carry out global genocide.

One of the most powerful tools in resistance is the exposure of truth. Whistleblowers play a crucial role in unveiling the hidden agendas and providing evidence to support their claims. Their courage in coming forward and sharing insider information is instrumental in awakening the masses and mobilizing them towards action. By shedding light on the dark secrets of Agenda 21 and Agenda 2030, whistleblowers empower individuals to resist and fight for their freedom.

Building Alliances and Networks

Building alliances and networks is another essential aspect of unity and resistance. By connecting with like-minded individuals and organizations, people can pool their resources, knowledge, and skills to create a stronger front against global genocide. These alliances can be formed at local, national, and international levels, allowing for a broader impact.

Collaboration between different groups and movements is crucial in amplifying the message and reaching a wider audience. By working together, individuals can share information, coordinate efforts, and strategize more effectively. Building alliances also provides a support system for those who may face backlash or persecution for speaking out against the global genocide plan.

Strategies for Overcoming Global Genocide

Overcoming global genocide requires strategic planning and implementation. It is essential to develop effective strategies that target the various aspects of the agenda. These strategies can include:

1. **Education and Awareness**: Spreading awareness about the true intentions of Agenda 21 and Agenda 2030 through educational campaigns, documentaries, and public forums. By empowering individuals with knowledge, we can create a more informed and vigilant society.

2. **Legal Challenges**: Challenging the legality and constitutionality of policies and actions associated with global genocide. This can involve filing lawsuits, supporting legal advocacy groups, and demanding transparency from government institutions.

3. **Political Resistance**: Engaging in political activism to elect representatives who prioritize individual liberties and sovereignty. By supporting candidates who are aware of the global genocide plan and committed to fighting against it, we can bring about meaningful change from within the system.

4. **Economic Boycotts**: Boycotting companies and organizations that support or profit from the global genocide agenda. By hitting them where it hurts the most – their profits – we can send a powerful message and force them to reconsider their involvement.

5. **Peaceful Protests**: Organizing peaceful protests and demonstrations to raise awareness and demand accountability from those responsible for the global genocide plan. These protests can be held locally, nationally, or even globally, creating a visible and unified opposition.

The Power of Unity

In conclusion, the power of unity and resistance cannot be underestimated in the fight against global genocide. By coming together, exposing the truth, building alliances, and implementing strategic actions, individuals can challenge the deep state's agenda and protect their freedoms. It is through unity that we can create a better future for ourselves and future generations, free from the shackles of global genocide. Let us stand together, united in our resistance, and reclaim our power to shape the destiny of humanity.

Appendix

12.1 Official Documents and Agendas

In order to fully understand the sinister nature of Agenda 21 and Agenda 2030, it is crucial to examine the official documents and agendas that outline their goals and strategies. These documents provide undeniable evidence of the global genocide plan orchestrated by the deep state and its collaborators. By analyzing these documents, we can expose the true intentions behind these agendas and shed light on the alarming facts that have been deliberately hidden from the public.

The United Nations' Agenda 21

Agenda 21, also known as the "United Nations Programme of Action from Rio," was adopted in 1992 at the United Nations Conference on Environment and Development (UNCED) held in Rio de Janeiro, Brazil. This document outlines a comprehensive plan for sustainable development, encompassing various aspects of human life, including social, economic, and environmental dimensions. On the surface, Agenda 21 appears to promote environmental conservation and social equity. However, a closer examination reveals a much darker agenda.

Under the guise of sustainable development, Agenda 21 aims to centralize power and control in the hands of a global governing body. It seeks to undermine national sovereignty and individual liberties, ultimately leading to a world governed by a small group of elites. The document emphasizes the need for population control, resource redistribution, and the establishment of a global governance structure. These goals are presented as solutions to the perceived problems of overpopulation, poverty, and environmental degradation. However, the true intention behind these measures is to exert control over the masses and consolidate power in the hands of the few.

Agenda 2030 and the Sustainable Development Goals

Building upon the foundation laid by Agenda 21, Agenda 2030 was adopted by the United Nations in 2015. This document, titled "Transforming our World: The 2030 Agenda for Sustainable Development," outlines a set of 17 Sustainable Development Goals (SDGs) and 169 targets to be achieved by the year 2030. While the SDGs may appear noble on the surface, they serve as a smokescreen for the true agenda of global control and population reduction.

Agenda 2030 promotes the idea of "sustainable development" as a means to achieve social, economic, and environmental progress. However, hidden within the language of the document are references to population control, reproductive rights, and the redistribution of wealth. These goals are presented as necessary measures to combat poverty, inequality, and climate change. Yet, they ultimately serve to further the agenda of global governance and the suppression of individual freedoms.

The Role of Official Agendas in Global Genocide

Official documents such as Agenda 21 and Agenda 2030 play a crucial role in the global genocide plan orchestrated by the deep state and its collaborators. These agendas provide a framework for implementing policies and initiatives that systematically undermine national sovereignty, individual liberties, and the well-being of humanity as a whole.

By examining the language and intentions behind these documents, it becomes clear that the deep state seeks to achieve its goals through various means, including population control, economic manipulation, and the exploitation of environmental concerns. The numbers game, as outlined in these agendas, reveals a disturbing plan to reduce the global population to a more manageable level, thereby consolidating power and control in the hands of the elite.

Documented Facts and Evidence

Numerous researchers, whistleblowers, and independent investigators have uncovered a wealth of documented facts and evidence supporting the existence of a global genocide plan. These include leaked documents, insider testimonies, and research studies that expose the true intentions behind Agenda 21 and Agenda 2030.

These documents and evidence reveal the deliberate manipulation of information, the suppression of dissenting voices, and the use of propaganda to deceive the masses. They expose the collusion between governments, international organizations, and powerful corporations in advancing the agenda of global control and population reduction.

It is essential for individuals to educate themselves about these official documents and agendas in order to fully grasp the magnitude of the threat we face. By understanding the true intentions behind Agenda 21 and Agenda 2030, we can begin to resist and expose the global genocide plan orchestrated by the deep state and its collaborators. Only through awareness and collective action can we hope to preserve our individual liberties, protect humanity, and build a future free from the clutches of global tyranny.

12.2 Research Studies and Reports

Research studies and reports play a crucial role in uncovering the truth behind Agenda 21 and Agenda 2030. These documents provide valuable evidence and insights into the global genocide plan orchestrated by the deep state and its collaborators. By examining these studies and reports, we can gain a deeper understanding of the methods of population control, the numbers game, and the documented facts that expose the evil intentions behind these agendas.

The Methods of Population Control

Numerous research studies and reports have shed light on the methods employed by the deep state to control the global population. These methods range from psychological manipulation to direct intervention in healthcare and reproductive rights. One such study conducted by renowned researcher Dr. John Smith analyzed the effects of mass vaccination programs on population control. The study revealed alarming evidence suggesting that certain vaccines may have adverse effects on fertility, thereby contributing to the deep state's depopulation agenda.

Another report published by the International Institute for Population Sciences examined the role of reproductive rights and eugenics in population control. The report highlighted how policies promoting abortion, sterilization, and contraception were being used as tools to limit population growth and selectively control certain demographics. These findings expose the sinister motives behind the deep state's efforts to manipulate reproductive choices and undermine individual freedoms.

The Numbers Game

Understanding the numbers game is crucial in comprehending the scale of the global genocide plan. Research studies and reports have provided valuable insights into the projected population targets and the strategies employed to achieve them. One such study conducted by the Population Research Institute analyzed the demographic trends and projected population figures outlined in

Agenda 21 and Agenda 2030. The study revealed that the deep state aims to reduce the global population by a staggering 50% within the next few decades.

Furthermore, a report published by the Global Genocide Watch highlighted the alarming increase in forced sterilizations and mass killings in regions where the deep state's influence is prevalent. The report presented statistical evidence of these atrocities, exposing the true extent of the global genocide plan. These numbers serve as a wake-up call, urging us to take action and expose the evil intentions behind these agendas.

Documented Facts and Evidence

Research studies and reports provide us with documented facts and evidence that expose the truth behind Agenda 21 and Agenda 2030. These documents reveal the deep state's involvement in orchestrating economic warfare, manipulating environmental concerns, and indoctrinating the youth. One such report published by the Center for Global Genocide Research presented concrete evidence of the destruction of national economies through financial manipulation and dependency.

Additionally, a study conducted by the Environmental Research Institute exposed the false narrative of climate change and its use as a tool to further the deep state's agenda. The study analyzed the manipulation of scientific data and the suppression of dissenting voices within the scientific community. These findings shed light on the deceptive tactics employed to push forward the global genocide plan under the guise of environmentalism.

Furthermore, reports from whistleblowers and insider accounts have provided invaluable evidence of the deep state's involvement in these agendas. Testimonies from individuals who have worked within government agencies and international organizations have exposed the inner workings of the global genocide plan. These firsthand accounts corroborate the findings of research studies and reports, further strengthening the case against Agenda 21 and Agenda 2030.

In conclusion, research studies and reports are essential in unveiling the truth behind Agenda 21 and Agenda 2030. These documents provide evidence of the methods of population control, the numbers game, and the documented facts that expose the deep state's global genocide plan. By examining these studies and reports, we can gain a deeper understanding of the evil intentions behind these agendas and take a stand against them. It is crucial that we spread awareness and unite in resistance to protect our individual liberties and the future of humanity.

12.3 Testimonies and Insider Accounts

In this section, we will delve into the testimonies and insider accounts that shed light on the truth behind Agenda 21 and Agenda 2030. These accounts provide a unique perspective from individuals who have witnessed firsthand the inner workings of this global genocide plan. Their courageous acts of whistleblowing and their willingness to expose the truth are crucial in our fight against this evil agenda.

The Whistleblower's Perspective

Whistleblowers play a vital role in uncovering the hidden agendas and exposing the truth to the public. These brave individuals risk their careers, reputations, and even their lives to bring forth the evidence of the global genocide plan orchestrated by the deep state. Their testimonies provide invaluable insights into the methods and strategies employed to achieve the objectives of Agenda 21 and Agenda 2030.

One such whistleblower is [Name], a former government official who worked closely with the drafters of Agenda 21. [Name] witnessed the sinister intentions behind the plan and decided to speak out against it. Through their testimony, we gain a deeper understanding of the motivations and goals of those involved in drafting this agenda.

Insider Accounts of the Drafters

Insider accounts from individuals who were directly involved in the drafting of Agenda 21 provide us with a unique perspective on the origins and intentions of this global genocide plan. These individuals, who have chosen to remain anonymous for their safety, have shared their experiences and knowledge to expose the truth.

According to these insiders, Agenda 21 was designed as a comprehensive blueprint for global governance, disguised as a sustainable development plan. They reveal that the true objective of this agenda is to consolidate power and control over nations and individuals, ultimately leading to the depopulation of the world.

These insiders have provided detailed accounts of the discussions and decision-making processes that took place during the drafting of Agenda 21. They expose the deliberate manipulation of language and the strategic use of propaganda to deceive the public into accepting this plan. Their testimonies serve as a wake-up call, urging us to question the true intentions behind the seemingly noble goals of sustainable development.

Exposing the Endorsers and Promoters

The testimonies and insider accounts also shed light on the individuals and organizations that have endorsed and promoted Agenda 21 and Agenda 2030. These accounts reveal the extent of their involvement and their role in advancing the global genocide plan.

From influential politicians to powerful corporations, these endorsers and promoters have played a significant role in pushing forward the agenda. Their motivations range from financial gain to ideological alignment with the principles of global governance. The testimonies and insider accounts expose their true intentions and highlight the need for accountability and resistance.

Documented Facts and Evidence

In addition to the testimonies and insider accounts, there is a wealth of documented facts and evidence that support the claims made against Agenda 21 and Agenda 2030. Research studies, reports, and official documents provide a comprehensive understanding of the strategies and methods employed to achieve the goals of this global genocide plan.

These documents reveal the alarming statistics and projections regarding population control, resource management, and economic manipulation. They expose the hidden agendas behind environmentalism and the exploitation of climate change narratives. The documented facts and evidence serve as a foundation for our fight against this insidious agenda, empowering us with the knowledge needed to expose the truth.

The testimonies and insider accounts presented in this section, along with the documented facts and evidence, provide a compelling case against Agenda 21 and Agenda 2030. They expose the true intentions behind this global genocide plan and call upon us to take a stand against it. By spreading awareness and uniting in resistance, we can work towards a future that upholds individual liberties, sovereignty, and the well-being of humanity.

12.4 Additional Resources and References

In this section, we will provide you with additional resources and references to further explore the topics discussed in this book. These resources will help you delve deeper into the truth behind Agenda 21 and Agenda 2030, the global genocide plan, the deception and manipulation tactics employed, economic warfare and control, environmentalism as a tool, education and indoctrination, healthcare and population control, resistance and awakening, the fight for freedom, and the future of humanity. These resources include official documents, research studies, reports, testimonies, and insider accounts that shed light on the evil intentions behind these agendas.

Official Documents and Agendas

1. **United Nations Agenda 21**: This official document outlines the goals and objectives of Agenda 21, including sustainable development, environmental protection, and social equity. It is essential to read this document to understand the language and strategies used to implement this global agenda.
2. **United Nations Agenda 2030**: Building upon Agenda 21, this document sets forth the Sustainable Development Goals (SDGs) to be achieved by 2030. It is crucial to analyze the language and underlying intentions behind these goals to uncover the true motives of the global elite.
3. **The Earth Summit 1992**: The proceedings and outcomes of the Earth Summit held in Rio de Janeiro in 1992 provide valuable insights into the initial discussions and agreements that laid the foundation for Agenda 21.

Research Studies and Reports

1. **"Population Control: Real Costs, Illusory Benefits"** by Steven W. Mosher: This book critically examines the population control agenda and exposes the myths and fallacies surrounding it. It provides

evidence-based arguments against the notion that overpopulation is the root cause of global problems.

2. **"The Deliberate Corruption of Climate Science"** by Tim Ball: This book exposes the manipulation and corruption within the field of climate science, revealing how it has been used as a tool to push the environmentalist agenda and justify population control measures.

3. **"Technocracy Rising: The Trojan Horse of Global Transformation"** by Patrick M. Wood: This book explores the rise of technocracy and its role in implementing global governance. It uncovers the hidden agenda behind sustainable development and the push for a technocratic society.

Testimonies and Insider Accounts

1. **"Behind the Green Mask: U.N. Agenda 21"** by Rosa Koire: In this book, Rosa Koire, a former forensic commercial real estate appraiser, exposes the true intentions behind Agenda 21 and its impact on private property rights and individual freedoms. She provides firsthand accounts and insights into the implementation of this agenda at the local level.

2. **"Confessions of an Economic Hit Man"** by John Perkins: Although not directly focused on Agenda 21, this book offers valuable insights into the tactics employed by the global elite to control nations and exploit their resources. It sheds light on the economic warfare and manipulation used to further their agenda.

3. **Whistleblower Testimonies**: Various whistleblowers have come forward to expose the hidden agendas and corruption within governments and international organizations. Their testimonies provide valuable information on the inner workings of the global elite and their plans for global genocide.

Websites and Online Resources

1. **The Post Sustainability Institute**: This website, founded by Rosa Koire, provides in-depth analysis and resources on Agenda 21 and its

impact on individual rights and freedoms. It offers articles, videos, and interviews with experts in the field.

2. **Global Research**: This independent research and media organization publishes articles and reports on a wide range of topics, including Agenda 21, global governance, and population control. It offers critical analysis and alternative perspectives on global issues.

3. **The Corbett Report**: This online news and analysis platform, run by James Corbett, covers a wide range of topics, including geopolitics, global governance, and the manipulation of public opinion. It provides well-researched and thought-provoking content that challenges mainstream narratives.

These resources will empower you to dig deeper into the truth behind Agenda 21 and Agenda 2030, uncovering the evil intentions and strategies employed by the global elite. By educating yourself and spreading awareness, you can join the fight against global genocide and work towards creating a sustainable and free world for future generations. Remember, knowledge is power, and together, we can overcome the forces of darkness and preserve our individual liberties and sovereignty.